When Sheep Attack

Finn Amaz 9/0   15.00

WWW.EPISKOPOLS.COM
Books for Clergy and the People They Serve

ISBN: 1-4515-1391-7
ISBN-13: 9781451513912

When Sheep Attack

Dennis R. Maynard

2010

PART ONE

WOULD I RECOGNIZE AN ANTAGONIST?

PART TWO
COULD IT HAPPEN IN MY
CONGREGATION?

PART THREE
CLERGY AND CONGREGATIONS ARE
DESTROYED

PART FOUR
AN OUNCE OF PREVENTION

PART FIVE
WHAT NEEDS TO HAPPEN?

PART SIX
LIFE BEYOND THE TOXIC PARISH

ACTION STEPS FOR CLERGY
AND BOARDS UNDER ATTACK

COVER DESIGN

I am grateful to Chris Koonce of Fort Worth, Texas for designing the cover to this book. He is a very talented young artist. Chris earned a Bachelor of Fines Arts degree in 1991 from the University of North Texas. I encourage you to visit his website to view his portfolio of artwork. There are several opportunities for personalized gifts for yourself and others. He can also be a resource for fundraising opportunities for your organization, parish or school. Please visit his website at:

www.kcfunart.com

BOOKS BY
DENNIS R. MAYNARD

THOSE EPISKOPOLS

This is a popular resource for clergy to use in their new member ministries. It seeks to answer the questions most often asked about the Episcopal Church. Questions like: "Can You Get Saved in the Episcopal Church?" "Why Do Episcopalians Reject Biblical Fundamentalism?" "Does God Like All That Ritual?" "Are There Any Episcopalians in Heaven?" And others.

FORGIVEN, HEALED AND RESTORED

This book is devoted to making a distinction between forgiving those who have injured us and making the decision to reconcile with them or restore them to their former place in our lives.

THE MONEY BOOK

The primary goal of this book is to present some practical teachings on money and Christian Stewardship. It also encourages the reader not to confuse their self-worth with their net worth.

FORGIVE AND GET YOUR LIFE BACK

This book teaches the forgiveness process to the reader. It's a popular resource for clergy and counselors to use to do forgiveness training. In this book, a clear distinction is made between forgiving, reconciling, and restoring the penitent person to their former position in our lives.

THE MAGNOLIA SERIES

BEHIND THE MAGNOLIA TREE (BOOK ONE)

Meet The Reverend Steele Austin. He is a young Episcopal priest who receives an unlikely call to one of the most prestigious congregations in the Southern United States. Soon his idealism conflicts with the secrets of sex, greed, and power at historic First Church. His effort to minister to those living with AIDS and HIV brings him face to face with members of the Klu Klux Klan. Then one of the leading members seeks his assistance in coming to terms with the double life he's been living. The ongoing ministry of conflict with the bigotry and prejudice that are in the historic fabric of the community turn this book into a real page-turner.

WHEN THE MAGNOLIA BLOOMS (BOOK TWO)

In this the second book in the Magnolia Series, Steele Austin finds himself in the middle of a murder investigation. In the process the infidelity of one of his closest priest friends is uncovered. When he brings an African American Priest on the staff those antagonistic to his ministry find even more creative methods to rid themselves of the young idealist. Then a most interesting turn of events changes the African Priest's standing in the parish. A young associate undermines the Rector by preaching a gospel of hate alienating most of the women in the congregation and all the gay and lesbian members. The book closes with a cliffhanger that will leave the reader wanting another visit to Falls City, Georgia.

PRUNING THE MAGNOLIA (BOOK THREE)

Steele Austin's vulnerability increases even further when he uncovers a scandal that will shake First Church to its very foundation. In order to expose the criminal he must first prove his own innocence. This will require him to challenge his very own Bishop. The sexual sins of the wives of one of the parish leaders present a most unlikely pastoral opportunity for the Rector. In the face of the ongoing attacks of his antagonists, Steele Austin is given the opportunity to leave First Church for a thriving parish in Texas.

THE PINK MAGNOLIA (BOOK FOUR)

The Rector's efforts to meet the needs of gay teenagers that have been rejected by their own families cast a dark cloud over First Church. A pastoral crisis with a former antagonist transforms their relationship into one of friendship. The Vestry agrees to allow the Rector to sell the church owned house and purchase his own, but not all in the congregation approve. The reader is given yet another view of church politics. The book ends with the most suspense filled cliffhanger yet.

THE SWEET SMELL OF MAGNOLIA (BOOK FIVE)

The fifth book in the Magnolia Series follows the Rector's struggle with trust and betrayal in his own marriage. His suspicions about his wife take a heavy toll on his health and his ministry. He brings a woman priest on the staff in face of the congregation's objections to doing so. Some reject her ministry totally. Then the internal politics of the Church are exposed even further with the election of a Bishop. Those with their own agenda manipulate the election itself. Just when you think the tactics of those opposed to the ministry of Steele Austin can't go any lower, they do.

THE MAGNOLIA AT SUNRISE (BOOK SIX) TO BE RELEASED FALL, 2010

The lives of The Reverend Steele Austin and the people of First Church face new challenges. Father Austin takes his sabbatical time to examine his life's purpose. Still stinging from the most recent attacks on his wife and himself from the antagonists in his congregation, he wrestles with the decision as to whether or not he wants to return to First Church. He is even uncertain if he wants to remain in the priesthood.

All of Doctor Maynard's books can be viewed and ordered on his website
WWW.EPISKOPOLS.COM

WWW.Amazon.com

Or Through Your Local Bookstore

BOOKS FOR CLERGY AND THE PEOPLE THEY SERVE

*With gratitude to the clergy that participated
in the research for this book.
Painful experiences can be
forgiven and healed, but they are seldom forgotten.*

Jesus said, "Behold, I send you out like sheep among wolves;
So be wise as serpents and innocent as doves."
Matthew 16:1

Introduction

Do you love your parish? Are you fond of your pastor? Would you believe that in just a matter of a few weeks your pastor and his family could be abused, humiliated, and unemployed? In just a matter of days your parish could be split down the middle. A couple of months from now close to forty percent of the people you currently see at worship could no longer be there. Close to half of those will never again attend worship or participate in any church. Friends that you see talking and laughing this Sunday may never speak again.

If you want to do whatever you can to keep that scenario from happening to your pastor and your parish, then this book is for you. It is the product of nearly a decade of work with parishes that are undergoing or have recently undergone the very scenario described above.

Because some readers may find the conclusions in this book disturbing, even shocking, I want to clearly state the methodology I used. The idea for this book came from my experience serving as a consultant to over one hundred congregations in the United States and Canada. The majority of the time, I was invited to do so by the rector or senior pastor. Those invitations came most often because **a small group in the parish was bullying them** and they hoped I could help them find an amicable way to work with them. The work crossed denominational lines to include clergy in the Episcopal, Lutheran, Methodist and The United Church of Christ. A few years ago I began to notice a distinct pattern of behavior in the various parishes. I became equally aware of certain characteristics in the congregations that appeared to contribute to the toxic behavior. It was almost as though I could tell the story in each parish by simply changing the names of the primary characters to protect the guilty.

In preparation for this book, I contacted forty clergy that had done battle with antagonists. At the time of the attack each was serving what can only be described as growing and dynamic congregations. The majority of their membership, their peers and their superiors would consider each of the forty clergy exceptional. All of them had chosen to end the fight with the antagonists by leaving their parishes. I asked them to complete a survey, repeat their story and help me build a case study of their experiences. I made provision for the surveys to be returned to me anonymously. While several chose to remain so the majority enclosed notes or letters encouraging me to contact them further if needed. It also needs to be noted that while I was the consultant to a handful of these clergy, I was not the consultant for the overwhelming majority. I was made aware of most of the clergy and their experiences by other clergy and lay people. I had no first hand knowledge of their experience.

Twenty-five surveys and case study stories were returned to me. In order to further gain clarification on some issues I followed up with telephone interviews to selected clergy who agreed to grant one to me. It needs to be noted from the beginning that I am uncertain as to which surveys were returned by women clergy since none of the women clergy I contacted identified their surveys for me. On the other hand, I have no reason to believe that the fundamental behavior patterns of the antagonists would be any different with a male or female clergy person. My routine use of *him* or *he* is done to avoid the clumsy he/she references.

I examined the surveys looking first for areas of unanimous agreement. I then looked for the areas agreed on by at least seventy-five percent of the clergy. These findings make up the substance of this book. While they may not be a common experience for all clergy and all congregations they are the reported experiences of these twenty-five clergy. If other studies are accepted, hundreds if not thousands of other clergy and congregations of all denominations have lived through a similar trauma. While recognizing that each priest's experience is unique there are so many ways their experiences replicated one another. One might even conclude that these clergy, unknown to each other, had identical traumas with different people in parishes separated by thousands of miles.

Based on these twenty-five case studies the following conclusions will become evident.

1. We can no longer afford the luxury of denying that there are dysfunctional personalities in congregations that want to hurt clergy.

2. Potential antagonists can be indentified by specific personality and behavioral characteristics.

3. The methods used by the antagonists to attack **clergy and divide congregations follow an identifiable pattern.**

4. The impact of these attacks on clergy, their families and the congregations they serve is devastating.

5. There are identifiable elements in the congregational system that allows the antagonists to do their toxic work.

6. There are positive steps that can be taken to make the congregation less friendly to the toxic element.

7. Ultimately, in order to neutralize the work of the antagonists all the "players" in the congregational system must work together.

I owe so much to so many. First, my heartfelt thanks to the vestries and clergy throughout the United States and Canada that have trusted me to serve as their consultant during some very difficult times in their lives. I've learned so much from each of you. With each consultation I've been able to sharpen my tools and my insights. I am especially indebted to all the clergy that completed the case study surveys and granted me follow up interviews in preparation for this book. I am grateful to you for your openness, your honesty and your trust.

All of the clergy that participated in this work continue to feel the repercussions of the nastiness heaped on them. It is important to recognize that these clergy did not leave their parishes because they are weak or they believed themselves to be in error. To the person they ended the battle because it was dividing their congregations. They did not want their parishes split any further. These clergy left their congregations not because they were bad pastors but the polar opposite. **They were being faithful shepherds that did not want to their flock to be completely ravaged.** They realized that the only way the people they were serving could move forward with forgiveness and reconciliation was if they were no longer in the mix.

Emotionally and physically, they did so because they simply ran out juice. They didn't want to fight any longer. **"I was exhausted"** was a common response. I am grateful to each of them for participating in this work, for their candor and their service.

I also owe a special word of thanks to **David Burgdorf of the Betty Ford Center** in Rancho Mirage, California. David's insights and guidance into understanding the behavior of those who live with addiction brought a critical light to this study. David also introduced me to other counselors at this incredible center of healing and recovery that provided me with additional understanding.

I am equally grateful to my friend of three decades, **The Right Reverend Ed Salmon.** To him and to the clergy he suggested I interview in the Episcopal Diocese of South Carolina I am deeply indebted for their contributions to this study. Bishop Salmon's particular contributions will become apparent as you turn the following pages.

To single out one particular mentor in my life is not an easy task. The teachings of each of the following mentors have indirectly contributed to the insights recorded in this book. However, in the area of congregational development there is no contest. **The Reverend Doctor Arlin Roth-**

uage first introduced me to the concept of congregational systems. Arlin has done so much not only for the Episcopal Church but also for the Church in the world. When he was the Congregational Development Officer for the National Episcopal Church he was the first to give us the concept of *congregational types*. He observed that congregations are not just larger sizes of one another. It was Arlin that taught us to think of the various sizes of congregations as being different functioning systems that have to be led in differing ways.

It was my pleasure to work with Arlin to develop two national conferences for multi-staff parishes. I was further honored to be able to work with Arlin and Bishop Mark Sisk, then Dean of Seabury Western Seminary, to expand the doctoral program at Seabury beyond the Chicago campus. I worked with them to design and begin a regional campus for doctoral studies in Houston, Texas. I was then appointed an adjunct member of the Seabury faculty in congregational development. Arlin's influence on my life and the way I think about congregational systems is unending. For this, I am so grateful.

While I cannot claim him as a long time mentor, I do want to acknowledge the work of **the late Rabbi Edwin Friedman.** His book, *Generation to Generation* (Guilford Publishing) was groundbreaking when it came to understanding family process in the congregation. It was my privilege to sit at his feet on several occasions. I value most the opportunities I was given to talk with him one on one or in a small group. I admired him for his ability to cut through the complexities and get to the bottom line. On one occasion I heard him respond to a question about a difficult personality, "Some people are just jerks!" On another in response to a question about a dysfunctional congregation, he asked, "Wasn't it your guy that said you need to know when to shake the dust off your feet?"

There are three laymen I want to acknowledge. I fear they have taught me more than I was able to teach them about congregational life. The insights I received from them are also reflected in this manuscript. The first is **Michael Foley** of La Jolla, California. Mike designed a system of internal financial controls for our parish that would be the envy of any enterprise. **David Ward, C.P.A**. also of La Jolla, California is a passionate accountant. Not only is he a person of incredible integrity, but also aggressively seeks the truth. For Dave, it's more than numbers. It's doing what's right. For that reason alone, he will always get to wear the super hero cape in my eyes. **Keith Kendrick** of Scottsdale, Arizona is one of the most insightful lay leaders I have ever worked with. He continually astonishes me with his ability to translate sound leadership principles to the operations of the parish.

There is one final clergy mentor that indirectly contributed to this work. I think I first attended a seminar being led by **The Reverend Canon William Geisler, C.P.A.** of San Francisco, California over twenty years ago. Since then I've attended several of his seminars and utilized his sound counsel and advice. He has taught me much about the financial operations of a congregation.

I've designed the book in such a manner that individuals can read it, but ideally it can be used on a weekend retreat with the church board, a clergy study or as the opening study at a series of board meetings. There are discussion questions at the end of each chapter.

If this book is used for group study I would like to recommend the following procedure. All the participants read a chapter. Then have a leader list on a grease board or newsprint the insights that the members would like to discuss further. The discussion questions at the end of the chapters can also be utilized. Following the discussion it is imperative that the group make a plan of action for the parish. This is a critical component. If no plan of action in each area is made, then this will just be one more study without the needed results that can make a real difference.

Dennis Maynard
Rancho Mirage, California
Easter, 2010

PART ONE
WOULD I RECOGNIZE AN ANTAGONIST?

Now the works of the flesh are obvious…enmities, strife, jealousy,
anger, quarrels, dissensions, factions, envy…and things like these.
Galatians 5:19-22

Chapter 1
They Create Malice in Wonderland

Father Tim was excited to receive the call to The Parish Church of Grace and Forgiveness. On his first Sunday he received a warm reception from the majority of the congregation. Still, he noticed that there was a handful that greeted him but not quite so warmly. He also noticed that these same folks had gathered in a tight knit circle at the coffee hour.

He didn't think much of it since he'd been told that the search committee and the vestry had been unanimous in their decision to call him as rector. It wasn't until a few weeks later that he would learn that neither had been unanimous and there was a segment of both that had fought for another candidate. The report of a unanimous decision was one that the bishop had forced on them.

Attendance at the Sunday worship services increased dramatically over his first three years. There was excitement in the parish. New ministry programs were being unveiled. For the first time in a decade the vestry was able to not only meet their projected budget but also make plans to increase it. Father Tim believed that the parish was responding to his leadership and God was going to do some great things in the congregation.

He had heard rumors that one of the retired associates in the congregation was not happy with him. The retired associate had befriended the newly employed young assistant. Father Tim had heard reports that they were being critical of his leadership and had even questioned his theology. Father Tim thought he just needed to give the two of them more attention and perhaps give them more time in the pulpit.

Then a strange thing happened. When the vestry met for their monthly meeting four members of the congregation joined them. They had some *concerns* that needed to be brought to the attention of the vestry. They assured the vestry that a great many members of the congregation shared these concerns. Their concerns ranged from questions surrounding the rector's use of church funds, to his leadership style and finally his work schedule. They had also heard that many in the parish did not believe that he was very pastoral. Others complained that he simply was not spiritual enough.

Father Tim tried to address each of their concerns at the meeting. Still, that night he had a difficult time sleeping. After his morning prayers he made the decision to work even more diligently at building up the parish.

He heard it first from his wife who had been advised of the happenings by a friend and supporter at a luncheon for the Women of the Church. It seems that there was a small group in the parish that were having a weekly cottage meeting. The retired associate was disguising them as Bible studies. The young assistant was also in attendance. Tim was confused by these rumors. Both priests pretended to be so warm and supportive of his ministry whenever he met with them.

The group had started an active email campaign to advise the parish of their unhappiness with the rector. The emails were extremely critical of Father Tim. They were filled with rumor and innuendo. The authors were all in agreement that Father Tim didn't preach the Bible. They had also circulated a petition and personally delivered it to the Bishop. They wanted the Bishop to remove Father Tim.

The small group continued to attend the monthly vestry meetings. Then the anonymous telephone calls began. There were harassing phone calls. Anonymous letters began to arrive that actually threatened Father Tim and his wife. Several even suggested that they had information on Father Tim and his wife that they would make public if he didn't resign. Gossip that Father Tim was having an affair with a woman in the parish spread through the community.

All this began to take a toll on both Father Tim and his wife. Their physician prescribed sleeping pills to help them sleep and an anti-anxiety medicine to help them make it through the day. One afternoon their son came home from school in tears. Some of the parish children that attended the same school with him had begun to bully him. They even told him that their daddy was a crook and that he was going to prison for misappropriating church funds.

Their son was unable to sleep at night and insisted on sleeping on the floor in his parent's bedroom. He did not want to go to school and tearfully begged his parents to transfer him to another school.

Somehow Father Tim continued to function even though his energy was low and he was becoming paranoid. He honestly didn't know which of the parish members were his friends and which were against him. Ironically, attendance at worship continued to grow. The Stewardship Drive for the next year exceeded all expectations. There were a handful of canceled pledges and another handful that pledged only one dollar a week. They had all noted on their pledge cards that they would not resume their normal giving until the current rector had been removed. Father Tim and the staff made plans to add an additional service on Christmas Eve. They were certain that the anticipated attendance would far exceed the seating capacity of the church.

The harassment accelerated as Christmas approached. He and his wife were both becoming more and more exhausted. They had to ask their physician for even stronger medications. Father Tim was gaining weight. His wife and his son on the other hand had to force themselves to eat. People had started to comment on just how heavy he was getting and that she was now much too thin.

The annual meeting was to be held on the second Sunday in January. In preparation for that meeting nominees for the vestry had to be made. The group that had been having the private Bible Study had nominated four of their members. They had been very vocal in their opposition to Father Tim and the need to have him removed. At the annual meeting of the congregation Father Tim noticed that there were people in attendance and voting that he had never before seen. They were successful in electing their nominees to the vestry. Some of those present at the annual meeting asked questions of the treasurer about the parish finances. While not accusing Father Tim of anything they suggested further investigation was in order. Similar questions were raised about his work schedule and his pastoral ministry. One person stated that he knew for a fact that the rector was not very supportive of the ministry of his staff and that his staff were actually afraid of him.

Father Tim's wife left the meeting in tears. Neither Tim nor she could figure out just what they'd done wrong. Except for a handful of people causing all the trouble everyone else in the parish appeared to be happy with them and Tim's ministry. In spite of the sleeping pills they both had a very restless night. They decided that they needed to get some counseling.

The next morning Father Tim received a telephone call from the Bishop. He appealed to the Bishop to intercede in the situation and to support him. Father Tim assured the Bishop that the majority of the parish supported him. There were only a handful of people trying to remove him.

Father Tim was shaken further by the Bishop's response. He suggested that for the sake of the parish and his own ministry he needed to "shake the dust off his feet and move on." The Bishop told him that he'd concluded that the only way that peace could be returned to the parish was for Tim to leave. The Bishop advised Tim that he would be sending his administrative assistant out to meet with him and the vestry to work out an agreement. The Bishop strongly encouraged Father Tim to cooperate and to be reasonable. If not, the Bishop would have to take steps to remove him. Two weeks later Father Tim signed the agreement and ended his ministry at The Parish Church of Grace and Forgiveness.

The Sheep Do Attack

Most of us would like to think that the above scenario is a work of fiction. The sad truth is that it is not. In one form or another this scenario is far too common. According to the work of **Gene Wood, author of *Leading Turn Around Churches*** (Church Smart Resources), 1300 Christian pastors are forced to resign their parishes **every month!** They are forced to do so without cause and often under a cloud of rumor and insinuation that will haunt them the rest of their ministry. Another 1200 hundred leave the ministry completely every month citing stress, church related issues, family issues, or burnout.

I'd like to think that "clergy under fire" is a contemporary phenomenon. However, my mind hearkens back to the days after my ordination forty years ago. I remember walking into the parish hall to teach a class and out of respect for my new station all in attendance stood. I remember thinking of the bishops of the church with a reverence best afforded the saints. Four decades have taught me that the winds of change have blown through the Church and not always with positive results.

Now, lest I overly romanticize the past I do have some other memories. I remember some of those in the little congregation that I attended as a teenager complaining that they needed a new preacher. "He's been here long enough," they would pronounce. "I don't care much for his preaching anymore," others would echo. "He doesn't visit the sick as often as he should," still others would proclaim.

I remember a local pastor that had become quite the radio personality in our little community. My grandmother would listen to his broadcast faithfully each Sunday evening. Even as a pre-adolescent I recall his deep and soothing baritone meditations. He had become somewhat of a local celebrity even with those who did not attend his parish.

He was often asked to say the invocation at community events. He was a natural for the baccalaureate sermon at the high school graduation. Then came rumors of a church fight. There were those who wanted him removed. He did resign and announced that he would reveal the names of the leaders that had led the charge against him during his next radio broadcast. While I have no evidence to substantiate this next assertion, I do remember that most everyone I knew tuned their radios to his final broadcast. Sure enough, he announced the name of five men in his congregation that had trumped up the charges against him to remove him from his pulpit.

I remember a conversation I had a few years ago with a private school consultant. He was lamenting the short tenure that heads of private schools were experiencing. Heads of schools were having shorter and shorter tenures. In just a matter of three or four years they were often under fire from parents and even their own faculties. He was working with a school in conflict over the leadership of the school head. He offered a rather simplistic explanation for it all. "These are the same people that twenty years ago as college students wanted to tell college presidents how to run their universities. Now as parents and teachers, they want to tell heads of school how to run their institutions. **We are dealing with a generation that believes they are the authorities in all areas despite the fact that they have no training or experience."**

Such an explanation could be transferred to the Church were it not for critical observation. Many of those that lead the charge against a priest are not products of the college campus of the sixties and seventies. Many are actually the parents of those same college students. So there must be another explanation for those who target perfectly capable clergy for removal.

The groundbreaking work of **Kenneth C. Haugk** in this area has to be noted. Pastor Haugk identifies what he calls *antagonists* in his book bearing that label in the title, ***Antagonists in the Church*** (Augusburg Fortress Publishers). While stopping short of describing them as suffering from a psychological disorder, their behavior pattern is easily discernible. These are people that thrive on creating trouble. They appear to have an insatiable need for power and control. Their reward is tearing down. The data in our twenty-five case studies could easily allow us to conclude that the more successful and popular the pastor the more likely they are to be attacked by the antagonists. But make no mistake about it. Their intent is to tear down both pastor and congregation. We could easily further conclude that their desire is to return the parish to its previous, less dynamic state.

I begin by accepting the premise that there are people that exhibit a behavior in the Church that can best be labeled as *antagonists*. I accept the premise that there are people who want to hurt clergy and return their parish to a place where they are both more visible and in control. It must be made very clear that the *antagonists* identified in this study are not to be confused with those that take an occasional "potshot" at the preacher. Nor are the *antagonists* described on these pages to be confused with those who offer positive critiques on ways that the parish ministry can be improved.

Clergy, like all leaders, need and want positive feedback. The *antagonists* that reap havoc on a pastor and a parish go directly for the jugular. They have a singular goal. They want to hurt, humiliate, destroy and remove the senior pastor. In the course of their attacks they want to intentionally divide the congregation between those that agree with them and the *supporters of the rector*. For all those reasons I will, without apology, use the word **antagonists** to describe these people and their behavior throughout this book.

My focus over these chapters will be on the areas of vulnerability for priest and congregation that most often become fuel for the antagonist. The old expression is that "only you can prevent forest fires." These case studies can lead us to conclude that there are certain safeguards that congregations can put in place to make themselves less friendly to the toxic element. Ultimately the best defense against a congregation being split by antagonists and having the ministries of faithful clergy destroyed rests with the manner the parish leaders, their senior pastor and the denominational authority respond to those orchestrating the attack.

For both clergy and laypersons that have lived through the attacks of the antagonists, much in this book will sound familiar. When a parish is being divided by these personalities there is little comfort in the knowledge that you are not the only one. What has been done is done. Most congregations spend decades trying to recover from the divisions caused by these people. Many formerly faithful members of the parish leave never to return to that or any congregation. Many of the clergy, their spouses and children will have nightmares of the vicious attacks until their dying day.

I once heard humorist Dick Gregory say, "Why is it that you can spot a street prostitute from a hundred yards away? You don't even have to ask her. Her actions and demeanor tell you she's a prostitute. But you can't spot some Christians until they tell you that they're one."

Antagonists, like the street prostitute, are easily spotted. They thrive on being critical. They enjoy conflict. They have extremely controlling personalities. They get their feelings hurt easily and turn those hurt feelings into anger, bitterness, resentment and ultimately revenge. **They are bulldozers fueled by a full tank of grudges.** They will take down anyone that gets in their way. They exist not to build up but to tear down. Their ultimate goal is the destruction of the shepherd. Like a dog with a bone, they will not let go of their grudge until they have their way. The tenacity of the antagonists and their energy for a prolonged battle was noted by several of the clergy in our case studies. As one priest noted, **"They were relentless. They simply wore us all out."** They smile only when the priest they envy or they believe has wronged them has been destroyed in the eyes of those who loved them. "By their works you shall know them." (Matthew 7:6).

Questions for Discussion and Reflection

1. Do you accept the author's premise that there exists in the Church characters that can appropriately be called *antagonists*? Why or why not?

2. Have you ever been in a parish that removed the rector or senior pastor? If so, describe that experience.

3. What happened to the rector? Where are they now? What are they doing? Do you know if the experience had any lasting impact on them mentally, physically, emotionally, and spiritually?

4. What was the impact on the parish? Attendance? Giving? Activity? Membership?

5. Which of the following do you think apply to the motivations of the antagonists? Envy/jealousy of the pastor? Control? Honestly believed they were doing what is best for the parish? Mentally/emotionally disturbed? Pharisees? Other?

    Throughout this book, rector and senior pastor are interchangeable terms. As are the words—vestry and church board, bishop and denominational authority.

When Sheep Attack

"Do not touch my anointed ones, and do my prophets no harm."
Psalm 105

Chapter 2
Unresolved Anger Driven By Control

From the very start of their ministry in the congregation all the clergy in our study reported that the antagonists attempted to control them. Some in our survey reported that there were attempts to renegotiate their letters of agreement after they took up residence. In particular, they wanted to lower the previously agreed on stipends and benefits. The majority of these clergy reported that these control efforts even expanded into their personal and family lives. There were efforts to put limits on their personal space including the location of their homes, the type of cars they should drive, the clubs they could or could not belong to, where their children were to go to school, where their spouse was to sit in church and even the number of services their spouse was expected to attend. A couple even reported that the antagonists wanted to dictate the type of clothes they were to wear and the length of their head or facial hair. Some even wanted to tell them when and how to smile when speaking to the congregation!

Follow up interviews with several of the clergy confirmed the feeling that it was **difficult to set boundaries with their critics.** Some literally wanted to tell them how to lead services. Others wanted to control their time in the office and just whom they were to visit in the hospital. There were demands that the senior pastor limit their involvement in the community or denominational activities. One rector actually received a telegram from a senior warden, one of his leading antagonists, instructing him to return home four days into his earned vacation. The senior warden stated in his telegram to the rector, "you have been on vacation long enough. It's time for you to come home and go back to work."

All but three of the clergy reported that they believed the antagonists wanted them to be subservient to them. In this same vein the vast majority reported that their attackers told them that they were their superiors socially and intellectually and therefore justified in treating them as they did.

All the clergy agreed that the antagonists were *arrogant*. Follow up interviews also found a consistent pattern here. The clergy believed that the antagonists wanted them to be **"their boy or girl."** They wanted them to be available to them 24/7 to do their bidding. Some even wanted to review and edit the priest's sermons each week before they were delivered. Still others wanted the priest to publish a daily accounting of their work schedule in the parish newsletter. The priest was expected to support their opinion and implement their advice as though it was a papal edict. Not to agree with them was not to love them.

It must be understood that those who attack clergy do so with one objective in mind. **Their goal is singular. They want the priest removed.** And if given the opportunity, they would destroy the priest's ministry completely. The nature of the attacks is rarely substantiated with any objective data. If the antagonists can't find actual financial wrongdoing they will then disagree with "how" funds are being used. Of course that means they are not being used the way they want. They will attack with phrases like "poor judgment".

The attacks on the clergy are relegated to subjective opinion. If the Sunday School attendance is up they will take issue with the curriculum being used. The most common attack reported in this study was on the clergy person's leadership style. They simply didn't like it. There were also attacks on their spirituality, they were not very pastoral, they didn't care for their preaching, or they were poor administrators. All of those are difficult to qualify. If the priest is a popular preacher they will take issue with the content of their sermons. They are either too liberal or too conservative depending on which will best serve their purposes. Even more injurious are the attacks that question the priest's honesty, trustworthiness, or their sense of calling.

A Sense of Entitlement

The clergy in our study all agreed that the antagonists operated from a *sense of entitlement*. They actually believed they were the most important people in the parish. They should be the decision makers for the entire congregation. A second line of agreement was that all the clergy noted that the antagonists held a total disregard for the feelings of those that disagreed with them. This is probably best illustrated by the comment made by one of the antagonists that had successfully worked to remove a senior pastor. **When asked just how many people he thought agreed with him that the rector should leave, he responded, "About 2%." Then he grinned and smiled, "But it's the right 2%."**

While it was not common to all twenty-five case studies, fifteen of the clergy noted that the leaders in the antagonists group had demonstrated symptoms of emotional instability. A couple had a history of mental illness. Unspecific anger in the antagonists was noted as the most common behavior characteristic. Or as one of our participants described, "They were just so angry. But their anger was so far out of proportion to the offenses they were accusing me of committing. I just couldn't figure out what was driving them."

When it comes to building a psychological profile of these people my research indicates that many do possess the characteristics applied to Narcissistic Behavior Disorder. The fact that they also possess high control needs would explain just why they exhibited volatile tempers. When people with high control needs believe they are not in control of a situation they become frustrated and explosive. Any person that refuses to submit to their demands will quickly become a target for their anger.

Just How Malicious Can They Get?

Things really get ugly when the attacks are personality oriented. These range from "she doesn't smile enough" to "the rector has anger issues." Four priests reported that the antagonists started rumors about the reasons for their previous marital breakups that had occurred decades ago. The antagonists had befriended one priest's ex-wife that he had divorced twenty plus years before and got her to join them in their attacks. Consider the time and energy required to first locate and then befriend a priest's ex-spouse. The ex-spouse was more than happy to unite with them in their cause. She was even successful in getting a retired and somewhat senile bishop that had sided with her in the divorce to write a letter the antagonists could use against the priest. He suggested in his letter, but offered no evidence, that the reason for the rector's divorce twenty years before was sexual misconduct.

The antagonists started **rumors of marital infidelity** about several of the priests in our study. This appears to be **one of the most frequently travelled avenues of maliciousness** for the antagonists. While they were unable to substantiate a single case, the damage done to the clergy marriages themselves cannot be ignored. When such rumors reached the ears of the spouse serious strain was placed on the relationship. Equally damaging were rumors started in two of our cases that the spouse was being unfaithful to her priest husband. In one case, the antagonists suggested that they had explicit pictures of the priest's spouse in an adulterous relationship with a single man in the community. They threatened to make them public if the priest did not resign. The answer to the question as to just how malicious the antagonists might get? As more than one of the clergy in our survey responded, "They knew the antagonists were willing to say and do whatever it took to get them to leave."

Dry Drunk

My suspicion is that if you are a reader with some knowledge of the addictive personality, the behavior described thus far is sounding familiar. People who live with addictions possess very high standards **for other people.** They are perfectionists, but it is a double standard. They ask perfection of others, but not themselves. Using the defense mechanism of projection, they can then put their own stuff on other people thus keeping them from having to look at their own.

If given the opportunity, one will discover that those with addictive personalities have a long list of grudges against people who have let them down. When anyone in their life fails to live up to their impossible standard of perfection they resent them for it. *The Big Book of Alcoholics Anonymous*, on page 64, includes this statement, **"Resentment is the number one offender. It destroys more alcoholics than anything else."** The addictive personality often masters the ability to harbor resentments.

Those who faithfully work the twelve steps of AA often find the fourth step to be challenging. It requires the individual to do a fearless moral inventory. In order to do that they have to move beyond their grudge list and take a hard look at themselves. They have to own their own stuff. Until they do there can be no forgiveness and they are simply unable to let things go. They will continue to nurture their grudges over and over again even years after the object of their resentment has long passed from this earth.

I recall one of the men in a parish I served that openly celebrated his thirty plus years of sobriety reminding me, "Padre, you can't look down on a drunk, because the drunk is doing too good of a job looking down on himself." What he also taught me was that the sense of shame and guilt was not realized until the person started owning their own stuff and stopped projecting it onto others. He stated, "A drunk is one of the best liars you'll ever meet. The tragedy is that until they stop lying to themselves they will never know serenity."

It should not surprise any of us to note that several of the clergy surveyed thought that their antagonists were alcoholics or possessed addictive personalities. "They just seemed so angry, bitter, even resentful" was repeated over and over again by the participants in this study. In preparation for this book, I've learned that just because an alcoholic has put the "plug in the jug" does not mean that they have achieved emotional sobriety. Those who work in recovery programs make a distinction between chemical sobriety and emotional sobriety. Those who have achieved chemical sobriety but have still not done their interior work are said to be on a *Dry Drunk*.

The characteristics of those on a Dry Drunk parallel those identified by our participants as those of their antagonists. High control needs, anger, resentment, envy and jealousy with an egocentricity verging on narcissism. Underlying this behavior is an unattainable standard of perfection for the person they choose to project all their resentments on. The obsessive-compulsive part of their personalities removes any possibility of forgiveness. They won't let go of any real or imagined wrongs done to them. Revenge becomes the driving force in their lives.

The insight that I have received in researching this book is that the behavior patterns of the *Dry Drunk* can and do occur in people who have no history of any substance abuse. Folks who have never done a thorough spiritual and moral inventory of their own lives get caught in the controlling behaviors that inevitably lead to anger, resentment, and revenge. Because they have not dealt with their own sins they become fixated on the real or imagined sins of others. The obsessive-compulsive part of their personalities makes it impossible for them to simply let go and move on. They will continue to nurture the real or imagined imperfections in another so they do not have to look at themselves. **In short, *Dry Drunk* behavior is possible in people who are chemically sober but still need to be healed spiritually themselves.**

Clergy become easy targets for these folks. They count on clergy being non-combative. They go for what they perceive as our weakness. Our message is one of compassion and forgiveness. Rather than confront, we seek to understand. Our goal is not to disenfranchise those who disagree with us but to try to find common ground. If they hurt us or they perceive that we have hurt them we seek forgiveness and reconciliation. Revenge is simply not in the clergy playbook. Those who want to hurt clergy count on using that to their advantage.

Questions for Discussion and Reflection

1. Have you ever known a person with high control needs? Did they try to control you? How did that feel? How did you respond to their efforts?

2. Are arrogant and controlling the same? Why? Why not? What do they have in common? Can you be one without being the other?

3. Have you ever been in a congregation where there were people that felt they were *entitled* to be in charge? How did you respond to them? How should a rector respond to them? Should the governing board defer to their wishes?

4. Why do you think "sexual misconduct" is one of the *favorite avenues of maliciousness* for antagonists? How effective do you think it is?

5. Reflect on the author's description of the "Dry Drunk." Are those characteristics transferable to the antagonists? Why? Why not?

6. Is there a relationship between doing one's own interior spiritual work and the ability to forgive others? Do you believe that people who have come to terms with their own imperfections are more accepting of the imperfections in others? Does this apply to clergy?

PART TWO
COULD IT HAPPEN IN MY CONGREGATION?

"Whatever town you enter, first say, 'Peace be to this house.' If a man of peace is there, your peace will rest on him; but if not, it will return to you. But whatever city you enter and they do not receive you, go out into its streets and say, 'Even the dust of your city which clings to our feet we wipe off in protest against you; yet be sure of this, that the kingdom of God has come near. 'I say to you, it will be more tolerable in that day for Sodom than for that city."

Matthew 10:11-15

Chapter 3
It's in the DNA

The majority of the clergy reported that the parishes they served had successfully removed one or more senior pastors in the past. This would correspond with other research in this area. **Parishes that have removed a rector in the past are most likely going to do it again.** Such behavior becomes a part of the congregation's DNA or internal system of operation. This DNA becomes even stronger when there has been a previous rector that has achieved the level of "beloved." Their presence becomes even more troublesome when they continue to attend the parish after their retirement. Their shadows often linger over the parish decades after their deaths.

Another critical component in the DNA of congregations inclined to remove clergy is a history of division. A congregation that has been divided over a rector in the past has a long memory and is quick to choose up sides if the opportunity presents itself again. My research also indicates that parishes with a history of division often take turns calling rectors. Obviously, the opposing side will never accept the rector that has been called by the other.

This is an alarming pattern when allowed to exist in the congregational system. In a parish with dueling clans, Clan A will call the new priest. Immediately Clan B rejects their choice and works to bring their choice down. Clan B then makes the next choice. Clan A rejects their choice and the pattern continues to repeat itself. Clergy who unknowingly get caught in this bear trap are like innocent sheep being led to the slaughter one after another.

I pursued evidence of previously removed clergy in telephone interviews with several of the clergy in this study. I asked them if they were aware of that toxic element in the history of the parish before accepting the call. Every one of them reported they knew. When asked why they then accepted the call anyway their answers varied. "I felt like they needed me." "I thought that I was a different kind of leader than the other rectors had been." "It was a larger assignment." "I never dreamed it could happen to me." "In the interview process the members of the congregation told me just how much they disliked the previous rector. That reinforced the feeling in me that I would be the exception and that they would really like me since I wasn't anything at all like that other guy."

Several years ago I was invited by the rector and two wardens (senior board members) in an Episcopal Church to consult with the rector and the staff. The rector was having a difficult time retaining his staff. He was curious, as were his wardens as to why he was continually losing staff. The high turnover rate had gotten the attention of the vestry and parish leadership. With the rector's permission I met with the staff without him being present. I learned that the staff members perceived him to be extremely controlling and that he possessed an explosive temper. Those two characteristics often go together. Their complaint was that he had a difficult time delegating and in their words "they never knew if they were going to be kissed or kicked" when they met with him.

When I asked him if he was aware of those perceptions he confirmed that he was. He sought to justify his behavior as an effort to make sure everything was done to perfection. He simply had no tolerance for mediocre work. I then met with the rector and wardens. My findings had confirmed their suspicions. They asked the rector if he would agree to go to a management-training seminar that focused on supervising staff. He agreed. They also asked him if he would agree to go to an anger management course. He agreed to that as well.

The senior warden drove me to the airport. I commended her for the lengths they were willing to go to assist their rector. I then asked the question that had been lingering in my mind. "Why are you doing this? I fear a lot of parishes would simply ask him to leave."

I will never forget the response. **"We don't allow our rectors to fail."** If only that healthy DNA could be implanted into every congregational system.

An Untouchable Staff Person

This just may prove to be one of the most disillusioning parts of this study, but one with a large red flag that must not be ignored. Every clergy person reported that they inherited an **"untouchable staff member often in the guise of an active retired clergy or a retired rector."** While some of the priests indicated on their survey that they knew that these individuals had actively worked for their removal, I followed up with others who indicated that while they did not know it for a fact they certainly suspected it. Only **one** of the twenty-five was confidant that a staff member had **not** undermined them.

These are not individuals that are "untouchable" because they are so incredibly gifted they would be impossible to replace. **They are untouchable because of the political alliances they've made with the "right people" in the congregation.** Most of the right people make up the toxic element in the congregation. This easily translates into a political chokehold on the parish.

Our survey participants reported that the "untouchable staff member" was not always a member of the clergy. These powerful staff people included long time secretaries, lay professionals, heads of parish schools and music directors. All had been in the parish long enough to build a separate group of followers that gave their loyalty first and foremost to that staff person. If the staff person chose not to support the senior pastor at any time, neither did their followers.

There is an old expression. *If the sheep are getting restless then a shepherd is stirring them up.* A definite part of this pattern in the case of clergy associates is that the priest or active retired associate had developed a pastoral ministry with an influential part of the parish to the exclusion of the rector. Tremendous persuasive power that can be used against the rector comes with such a position. These pastoral associates, both active and retired, so coveted the power and adulation that comes with an exclusive pastoral ministry that they had actually been able to shove the rector aside. This also placed them in the perfect position in the parish system to use their followers to work against the rector if they chose.

There is one question that this study was not able to completely resolve. Does the initiative for the attacks against the senior pastor originate with the clergy staff member or with the antagonists? Motivated by jealousy, theological differences or political ambition do the associates literally stir the antagonists into action? Or, do the antagonists triangulate with the clergy associate and draw them into the battle? As one of our participants described it, **"the retired priest enjoyed the adulation he got by stoking the fires against me."**

I've examined parish registers that showed that the rector of the parish performed very few of the baptisms, weddings, or funerals. Even more telling are the records that show that practically none of the funerals were preached and presided over by the rector of the parish. These were presided over and preached primarily by an active or retired associate. Would it surprise you to know that in my consultations more often than not it was the active or retired pastoral associate that was the chaplain to the antagonists intent on tearing down the rector? If not, then it won't surprise you to learn just whom the antagonists wanted to be named as the next interim or possibly permanent rector.

The members of the congregation may never remember a single sermon that a priest preached. It is certain they won't want to reminisce about the various committee and board meetings. They will, however, remember forever when their pastor visited them when they were sick, comforted them when grieving, and celebrated their joyous occasions with them. This is the power of the pastor. Clergy must be first and foremost pastors to their sheep. The faithful will come to the defense of a rector that has been their pastor more readily than other aspects of ministry. The antagonists will have a difficult time sowing seeds of discontent with people who have a pastoral relationship with their priest. There is the little pearl of wisdom, "People may never remember what you said but they will always remember how you made them feel."

While rectors of large parishes with multiple staffs cannot pastor everyone in the parish, it is essential that they have an active and faithful pastoral ministry with the leaders of the congregation. It is equally important that it be understood that the rector or senior pastor has the prerogative to preside at and preach any service of their choosing and that the associate defer with grace.

One of the biggest obstacles keeping **a new rector** from becoming the primary pastor in a parish is the existence of such a clergy person that already has the exclusive rights to that ministry. More often than not they are hesitant to relinquish or even share their pastoral privilege with the new rector. The end result is that the new rector never gets to be the pastor to the parish and thus becomes an easy target for the antagonists.

The Methods Utilized By the Antagonists

The antagonists have a large and destructive arsenal. The weapons they used against every priest in our case studies became quite predictable. The antagonists attended vestry and board meetings to bring their *concerns*. The word *concern* is a favorite of the antagonist. Complaints to the bishop, complaints to the members of the vestry, emails and letters to church members in which they shared their concerns were tactics reported by every priest in our study. They began their campaigns by **verbalizing their complaints to everyone but the senior pastor.**

There are two weapons in the war chest of the antagonists that are utilized with great effectiveness. These are the widespread use of **anonymous rumors** and **triangulation**. One of the most effective ways to disarm the antagonists and protect both your priest and your parish from their attacks is to expose both of them.

All the players in the congregational system (Bishop, denominational authorities, senior pastor, staff, wardens and board members) must agree that *anonymous reports* **are nothing more than malicious gossip.** They are never to be accepted as fact and therefore never repeated. Phrases such as "people are saying" or "I can't tell you who" are out of order. People must own their own *concerns.* They cannot hide behind the veil of anonymity.

A covenant refuting *triangulation* needs to be made in writing with all these same people and renewed on an annual basis. The covenant simply states that each signer will not participate in any third party conversations. If a concern or complaint needs to be heard the object of the complaint must be present. The Bishop and diocesan executives must make it clear that they will not accept telephone calls or visits from anyone with complaints about their senior pastor without including that senior pastor in the conversation.

This same covenant must include the wardens and all board members. They too must let the congregation know that the rector must be included in any conversations that have him as the object of concern. This will also prevent the bishop and board members from becoming unknowing but irrevocable partners with the antagonists in opposition to the rector.

In the corporate world there is the understanding that a large attendance at the stockholders meeting is not a good sign. The annual meeting in the parish is a favorite platform for the antagonists. Tremendous energy goes into gathering the crowd, but before gathering them they must first make sure they enter the meeting with a full head of steam. The antagonists have perfected the ability to upset the sheep. This is usually done through "secret meetings," email campaigns, and letters to selected members of the parish. Anonymous rumors and triangulation are the fuel that drives the anger.

Using the Election Process

Several of those surveyed reported serving congregations that elected the parish wardens at the annual meeting. The antagonists used this process to their advantage. In the majority of the congregations in the American Episcopal Church the rector appoints the senior warden from the elected vestry. The vestry elects the Junior Warden from their own number. When these two offices are elected by the congregation at the annual meeting the antagonists can go to great lengths to see that one of their number is elected to each position. Thus, the strongest voices in opposition to the rector become the senior members of the vestry.

Every congregation and bishop must ask themselves if the system in their particular parish is designed to encourage their senior pastor to have a long and successful ministry. Or are there elements in play that will lead to their inevitable failure? One priest reported that at his service of installation as the new rector his wife overheard one of the leading members of the congregation report to another, "There he goes. Our next sheep to be led to the slaughter." Does your parish system contribute to the success or failure of your rector and consequently that of your congregation? The answer to that question just may be in your history.

৵৽

Questions for Discussion and Reflection

1. Do you accept the author's premise that some parishes have it in their DNA or congregational system to allow antagonists to attack their senior pastors? Do you know such a parish? Have you ever been in such a parish? Describe their history.

2. Do you really think the antagonists want to control their pastor? Why or why not?

3. What objective criteria do you use to determine if your rector is being faithful to her ministry?

4. How does your parish elect the two senior officers or wardens of your vestry or board? What is good about that method? Can the antagonists use it?

5. Do you think the antagonists ever feel any shame or guilt about the way they treated a priest and his family? Do they suffer remorse for the damage they have done or do they try to justify it?

6. Do you know a priest that antagonists from a past parish have tried to destroy? Share that experience.

7. How should the board respond to antagonists when they have successfully triangulated with the bishop against the rector?

8. What can a board and senior pastor realistically expect a consultant to do for them in one of these situations? The bishop? An attorney?

"Why do you look at the speck of sawdust in your brother's eye and pay no attention to the plank in your own eye?"
Matthew 7:3

Chapter 4
Define Naughty

Santa Claus keeps two lists—one for the naughty children and one for the nice. It needs to be said up front that antagonists keep only one list. And they delight in finding items to add to their target's naughty list. Conflict often arises around a definition of naughty.

There are basically five levels to the conflict pyramid. At the very base of the pyramid is the first level, which I label **Facts.** Facts are based on verifiable data. When there is disagreement or conflict the data can be examined in an objective fashion so as to resolve the dispute. The *concern* is that the rector is not making enough hospital visitations. An examination of the rector's calendar can determine if that is in fact true.

Opinion is the second layer in the conflict pyramid. This is a bit more subjective. Differences of opinion require good listening skills and charity. It is entirely conceivable that two people can be looking at the very same thing, both see something different and both are absolutely correct. In order to resolve the conflict of opinion each party must listen to the other to gain insight into just why they feel the way they do. It could be that they will simply have to agree to disagree and in charity resolve to continue to work together.

The third level in the pyramid is **Innuendo.** Now the conflict becomes much more personal and therefore personality driven. Motive is assigned to the actions or non-actions of another. *The rector does not make enough hospital calls because he is lazy. She did not go to see my mother because my mom doesn't give enough money to the church.* When motives are assigned it is much more difficult to find a resolution without apologies, forgiveness and reconciliation.

Accusation is near the top of the pyramid and constitutes the fourth level. At this level the innuendo has become gangrenous and often involves labeling and name-calling. *The rector doesn't visit in the hospitals enough because he's un-pastoral. Or he's not spiritual enough. He really doesn't care about us. He is cold and uncaring.* Or in today's political climate the labels liberal and conservative can be used to justify dismissive feelings. *She didn't visit my mother in the hospital because she's a liberal and she knows my mother is a conservative. She's homophobic or he's just too liberal for me. She's not trustworthy. She's a liar.* At this level it is most difficult to find a resolution. When the attacks become personal and labels begin to be applied it is but a short step to the next and final level at the top of the pyramid – **Removal.**

Antagonists move up the conflict pyramid very quickly. They have no interest in dialogue, compromise, forgiveness or reconciliation. Their goal from the beginning is the removal and often the destruction of the rector. One of the most revealing ways to determine if the parish is in a resolvable conflict is to determine if the battle is being fought at the first two levels. At these levels a consultant can be used successfully to bring peace and resolve any issues. However, there is little hope for a happy resolution to the conflict if it has escalated to innuendo and accusation, even if the accusations are false. The only way that issues at this level can be resolved is through either the removal of the rector or the persons making the charges. Antagonists will begin at the innuendo and accusation level. They move quickly to removal.

One of the most revealing questions that can be asked is "What?" What do you want the rector to do? What can she do to please you? What can he do to make you happy? What is it they are doing that displeases you? What are they not doing? Asking "what" is not only a powerful question, but also it will quickly reveal the motives of the complainer.

As was pointed out earlier, our study indicates that often a member of the clergy or church professional is leading the antagonists. We have documented cases where one of the associate clergy was actively working with the antagonists to unseat a rector. On occasion these have been former rectors or associates that have long since retired but remain active in the political life of the parish. While this is disappointing and may be a real eye-opener for the faithful it has to be recognized.

One further reality must be acknowledged. **Bishops and other clergy are not immune from the sin of envy.** While those devoted to their particular bishop or pastor would prefer to see us as beyond temptation and sin, it's good to remember that we lead you in the confession at each Eucharist. Ordination does not vaccinate clergy, regardless of title, from sin. Clergy eyes can turn green over another's accomplishments. Theological differences can be bitter. Political rivalries can be divisive.

Motivated by jealousy over another priest's apparent success, political or theological differences, antagonists can recruit neighboring clergy or denominational executives and bishops to partner with them in their efforts to tear a priest down. One of our participants included a copy of a letter they had received from their bishop. In the letter the bishop complained that the priest's salary and benefits exceeded his own. He wanted the rector to voluntarily reduce his compensation and give the difference to the diocese.

Finding the Achilles Heel

Our research has discovered that antagonists will go to great lengths to investigate their target. Phone calls, emails and even visits to a priest's former parish, bishop, or school are a common activity of those intent on tearing that priest down. Searching through a clergy person's past looking for even the slightest rumor of any impropriety is a common activity of the antagonists. Random telephone calls to members of a priest's former parish were reported. Telephone calls to former bishops and neighboring clergy were also documented. Some in our study reported the antagonists actually traveled great distances to visit a clergy person's former parish. The quest was for any innuendo that could be placed under the spotlight.

One often mentioned method of attack by our participants was the priest's theology or Biblical beliefs. We don't burn people at the stake for heresy anymore, but there are plenty of clergy that have been attacked by antagonists for their theology and/or spirituality. "They don't preach the Bible" is a common assertion made by antagonists. Yet another, **"They are not very spiritual."** One retired priest actively sought to remove the new rector on the grounds that he did not preach that the unrepentant would go to hell.

Homosexuality and the ordination of women have been two controversial issues that clergy have had to confront in today's Church. Regardless of the position that one takes there will be members of the parish that take the opposing understanding. Clergy that take a traditional stand will disenfranchise the gay and lesbian members of the congregation, their families and friends. Those who speak a strong message of support risk losing the support of those holding the opposing view. This is fertile ground for antagonists. If they can rally the troops around an issue that appears virtuous it can serve as a smoke screen for their real goal. Evil is never so dangerous as when it disguises itself as good. Make no mistake about the objective. Their goal is to tear down the rector and the parish.

One of the more common accusations reported in this study was that their rector was not spiritual enough. Again, if the antagonists can paint the priest as a worldly person in love with the creaturely comforts, their accusations take on the guise of a holy mission. There were instances where the antagonists successfully froze a clergy person's salary or even caused a reduction in salary because they were seen as being "too worldly."

There is yet one more arena that is a fertile field for the antagonist. While there is no perfect person and we all have character and personality flaws, antagonists delight in magnifying the imperfections of their priest target. I remember standing near a rector that was shaking hands with his congregation after the service. He'd just preached what I considered to be a marvelous sermon. I was standing in line to thank him for his message. The lady in front of me approached him and said in a voice loud enough for all to hear,

"Did I hear a dangling participle in that sermon?" While she may not be an antagonist but a retired English teacher, such is the work of antagonists. They will miss all the good in favor of exaggerating what they have determined is a flaw. Remember, their goal is not to build up, but to *tear down*.

The list of potential character flaws is unending and as familiar as a close look in any of our mirrors. The antagonists refuse to deal with their own flaws by demanding perfection in their priest. As long as they are able to stay focused on their priest's failure to achieve their impossible standards they don't have to consider their own.

When attacked our natural response is to try to defend ourselves. This only brings smiles to the faces of the antagonists. One of the most disarming things that a priest can do when it comes to their human flaws is to be able to laugh at themselves. In the case of the English teacher pointing out the dangling participle, the rector smiled at her and chuckled; "I knew you were going to be here so I threw it in just for you."

Anxiety

Anxiety is the fuel of the antagonists. Anxiety is defined as an irrational fear of the unknown. The problem with antagonists is that you literally never know what they are going to do next. They plot and plan in the dark. They use the elements of secrecy and surprise to their advantage. They play by their own rules. As one member of a congregation so divided once observed, **"We knew they'd do whatever it took to get rid of our priest.** They were going to stop at nothing. We just didn't know how far they would go before he would decide to stop fighting with them."

If the antagonists can create an atmosphere of **"fear of the unknown"** in the priest and congregation they are in control. If they can create this same anxiety in the clergy spouse and children it enhances their power dramatically. They are in control of the forthcoming grass fire. The priest, spouse, parish leadership and often the bishop are on the defensive. But their defensive position is difficult to maintain because they don't know just what the antagonists will do next.

It is imperative that when under attack that the priest and the parish leadership not get caught up in the anxiety. It is essential that they remain calm, deliberate and intentional. As long as the conversation can remain rational and objective, the priest and leadership communicate to the parish that they are in control and not the antagonists. If the parish becomes anxious then the end result is predetermined. The antagonists know this!

It Only Takes Four or Five

One of the most revealing pieces of information this study discovered was that it only takes four or five ringleaders to completely divide a parish and bring down a priest. These ringleaders only need to recruit another dozen or so followers to accomplish their goal. As has already been observed, the denominational authorities and the healthy parish leaders more often than not **simply allow the 2% to run over the wishes of the 98%.** Unless the denominational leaders and the healthy parish leadership are willing to be firm with the antagonists, both their priest and their parish will be destroyed.

It is imperative that the leadership at all levels insist that the conversation be conducted on the first level of the conflict pyramid and not the upper ones. Facts must be the substance of the day and not rumor and innuendo. The leaders of the parish must be willing to lose a few in order to retain and gain the many.

I worked with one congregation that was being so divided. The attacks on the priest were unsubstantiated, but the entire congregation was in upheaval. I was able to determine not only the number but also the names of those that had been meeting with the retired associate to plot the downfall of the rector. With the rector's permission I was able to get the treasurer to give me the total of the contributions to the parish the group had made over the past year. The grand total was 156.00 dollars.

I presented that fact to the vestry. A dozen people who had each given an average of fifteen cents a week to the parish over the past year were trying to destroy the rector and divide the congregation. The majority had actually given nothing at all. I wish I could tell you that piece of information motivated the leadership to deal with them firmly. I regret I cannot. They succeeded to unseat the rector and divide the parish. And that, my friends, is a sad fact.

Questions for Discussion and Reflection

1. Share your impressions of the conflict pyramid. Share your own examples for each level of criticisms of a pastor.

2. How can you respond to the criticism that it's not what they have done but it's how they did it?

3. Do you think asking "what questions" is a good way to redirect the conversation to the first level of the pyramid?

4. How did you respond to the study's findings that ordained priests and bishops can join forces with antagonists to bring down a priest and divide a parish?

5. What are some of the things that a priest and parish leaders can do to keep from being caught up in the anxiety being created by the antagonists? In the face of anxiety, how can those under attack communicate to the parish that they are not anxious?

6. Respond to the finding that as few as four or five people can bring down a priest and divide a parish?

7. How do you think the bishop and parish leaders should have responded to the knowledge that the total giving in the one example by the antagonists was fifteen cents a week? Why do you think that in face of that fact the antagonists were still successful?

8. Understanding that most every congregation has a mix of people in it with differing understandings of sexuality, how can your rector "handle" this issue without becoming a target for the antagonists?

PART THREE
LIVES OF CLERGY AND CONGREGATIONS ARE DESTROYED

"Blessed are you when men give you a bad name, and are cruel to you, and say all evil things against you falsely, because of me."
Matthew 5:11

Chapter 5
The Sacrifice of the Innocent

There were two heartbreaking discoveries in this research. The first was the emotional, physical and spiritual damage done to the priests and their families by the antagonists. The second discovery was just how devastating the work of the antagonists is on so many members of the congregation. The physical, mental, and spiritual health of the clergy was injured. But so too were the lives of the members of the congregation that were devoted to their senior pastor.

Impact on the Clergy

One priest that had been removed from his parish over ten years ago has suffered such severe bouts of depression that he has been in and out of psychiatric hospitals several times. The final insult came recently when his wife of twenty plus years divorced him. Three of the priests reported **stress related heart attacks**. Seven acknowledged that they were diagnosed with **hypertension** and one priest had suffered **multiple strokes** that left him with physical challenges he must live with to this very day.

Every priest reported that the experience of being attacked by the antagonists had a negative impact on them physically, mentally, emotionally, and spiritually. Their descriptions ranged from battle fatigue to severe illnesses. Most all reported suffering from depression. Others described the emotional impact as feeling broken, defensive, withdrawn, fear, panic, a loss of creativity, energy and profound sadness.

All reported that the experience had impacted them spiritually. These responses ranged from questioning their abilities to questioning their call to ministry. Only one reported that they could find spiritual strength in the experience by identifying with the sufferings of Christ.

Impact on Clergy Marriages and Families

While a couple of the clergy in this study reported that their families went through the experience without any lasting consequences, the majority told a different story. There were stories that their spouse became the target of verbal abuse and gossip. In some of the cases the children were subjected to taunting by their schoolmates after being coached by their antagonist parents.

Most of these clergy spouses, and in some cases the children, had to seek psychological counseling and were prescribed prescription medications to help them deal with the experience. So severe was the strain on a few of the clergy spouses during the peak of the attacks that there were reports in our study of spousal adultery. These marriages ended in divorce. One of the spouses attempted to justify her actions "as striking out at her husband for getting her in this mess"

Our study also showed that some clergy spouses became addicted to prescription medications that had been prescribed to help them through the parish trauma. Others reported that their spouses had threatened to divorce them if they did not get them out of the parish and away from "those people". Three of the twenty-five clergy marriages in our study did end in divorce. The majority of the clergy reported that both they and their spouses had been diagnosed with **Post Traumatic Stress Syndrome** and have had to continue in treatment for years after the experience ended.

This sadness is only compounded by the fact that the majority of these clergy report that following the experience their spouses and one or more of their children will **no longer attend a church of any kind**. This is compounded further by our clergy participants who themselves report that their participation in any parish or Church life is now rare to never. The antagonists who targeted some of the clergy in our study were successful in destroying the very spiritual foundation in the Church that was a vital part of these marriages and families. The trauma of doing battle with the antagonists is not only felt by the clergy but by their families as well.

Before continuing, let me reiterate that in not one single case had any of the priests done anything that would have been considered criminal in a court of law. By the same token, none of them had done anything that would bring them before an ecclesiastical court for discipline. While none had done anything criminal and none were subjected to canonical discipline, rumors filled with innuendo and accusation will haunt some of them the rest of their ministries.

For Some It Did Not End

The antagonists in the majority of the cases were not content to simply have the priest removed. They continued to try to destroy their ministries years and even decades later. The majority of the clergy reported that the antagonists continued to defame them to the leaders of any new congregations they served or sought to serve. The antagonists were not at all hesitant to even work to keep them from securing new positions or destroy their ministries after they had secured a new position. Their attack continued in the form of letters, emails, and even visits to the priest's new parish. The majority of the clergy reported that choosing to end the battle with the antagonists and leave their parishes had injured their possibilities as a candidate for other positions in the church.

Antagonists destroyed the hopes for several of our participants to be elected bishop. The antagonists contacted the officials in the pursuing dioceses and defamed their former priest, thus insuring that they could not be further considered or elected. Sadly, in each reported case none of those diocesan officials contacted the priest or the healthy leadership in their congregations to discern if the accusations were true. They chose rather to believe the antagonists and remove the priests from further consideration.

Impact on the People in the Parish

Before considering the negative impact the battle had on the parish, let's review the state of the twenty-five congregations at the time the antagonists accelerated their attacks. In response to our participant's leadership each congregation had experienced an increase in attendance and financial giving in each parish. Likewise there was an air of excitement with increased activity at parish events up until the conflict began. **All twenty-five participants were**

serving congregations that were alive and growing at the time the antagonists accelerated their attacks on them. The clergy reported they had just completed the most successful stewardship campaign in the history of the congregation. Others had just conducted successful capital campaigns. Still others had just finished a successful building project or were about to embark on one. Record attendance at worship was being recorded and the rector, the parish or both had received national attention in the denominational press.

Perhaps the universal frustration for all the clergy is summarized in this statement by one of the priests. "I still don't know what I did wrong. Everything was going so well. Then a group of no more than a dozen people brought it all to an end. I just don't get it. Dennis, I hope your study will help me understand. **I feel like I was being punished for doing a good job.** Am I wrong? I loved my parish. I loved the people. My ministry with them energized me. Please, somebody tell me what I did wrong."

Every congregation experienced negative repercussions when the priest left the parish. The negative impact on the parish was seen immediately. Attendance and giving decreased dramatically. Membership declined and program growth became stagnant to non-existent. Empty pews at Sunday worship and declining parish collections were the most noticeable consequences. On average, 28% of the worshippers left these parishes and united with another. **19% left the parishes completely and have yet to return to that parish or any other.**

Only 35% of the membership remained as members in good standing, maintaining their giving and attendance. 38%

of those that remained decreased their financial support and activity in the parish. Another 18% remained on the membership rolls but became inactive.

Of the congregations in this study, this means that the wounds inflicted on the parish itself by *removing* a senior pastor result, on average, in an active membership loss of nearly one half. Even more tragic are the formerly active and excited Christians that become apathetic to the Church in general and leave never to return to any church.

Efforts to Disguise the Negative Impact

In an effort to disguise the negative impact on the congregation, the remaining leadership will often reduce the number of worship and program offerings. For example, a parish that formerly offered three services now offers only two. **The thought is that one or two reasonably full services sends a better message than trying to maintain the three or four filled by the departing rector.** While this may work psychologically for a short while, the total attendance enjoyed in the previous worship schedule is greatly reduced. Comparing the annual year-end reports against one another easily evidences this.

The parishes in our study faced yet another obstacle. **It took between eighteen months and five years before they were able to call another rector or senior pastor.** The average length of time that these parishes required to find another rector was three years. Most of these parishes have not yet returned to the attendance and giving levels they enjoyed prior to the trauma of battling with a group of antagonists.

Mediocrity Vs. Dynamic Growth

While it was not universal several of our participants noted that they believed that returning the parish to its former state of mediocrity was what they thought the antagonists really wanted. They observed that the antagonists often objected to the increase in attendance and new members. They resented the expanded program. **They particularly objected to having new leadership raised up in the congregation.** Once the parish is returned to its former size and activity the antagonists are in a better position to, as one priest wrote – "run things themselves".

As I've reviewed the twenty-five case studies two questions kept coming to mind. Clearly, these attacks had nothing to do with the quality of the work these clergy were doing. The attacks had nothing to do with the fruits of their ministries. Every congregation wants increased attendance and stewardship. Every congregation wants a renewed vitality with expanded programs. And certainly, every congregation wants to welcome and raise up new leadership among the members. Or do they? The lingering questions—could the very fact that these clergy are gifted leaders be the very reason for these attacks that clearly were so personal? Did the antagonists resent and even hope to destroy the many good things that were happening in these congregations? Sadly, the answers to those two questions can only be speculative and not conclusively drawn from this research. They do however…linger.

ॐॐ

Questions for Discussion and Reflection

1. Do any of the common threads experienced by all the priests in this study surprise you? If so, which ones? Why?

2. Since the parish will suffer negative repercussions by removing a priest, do the bishop and vestry have a responsibility to make sure that does not happen? How do you think the bishop and vestry should respond to the behavior of the antagonists?

3. Have you ever been in a parish that had an "untouchable staff or clergy person?" What was that like? Did that person support the rector or work against them?

4. Do you consider the rector to be the pastor of your parish? If not, then who?

5. Do you agree that an "untouchable" staff or clergy person, active or retired, could place a senior pastor in a difficult position? How should such a person be managed? If they are a retired clergy person, does that complicate the picture?

6. Discuss the merits of this statement, "Sometimes you have to lose a few to gain the many".

7. How do you think your vestry would respond to the efforts of antagonists to remove your current rector?

8. How would you answer the two lingering questions the author asked in the closing paragraph of this chapter?

PART FOUR
AN OUNCE OF PREVENTION

"*The one who listens to you listens to Me.*
The one who rejects you rejects Me; and he who rejects
Me rejects the One who sent Me."
Luke 10:16

Chapter 6
Every Parish Is Vulnerable

While the toxic characteristics favorable to antagonists were found in the parishes we studied, it would be foolish to think that any congregation is immune from the work of the antagonists. People are complicated. Congregations are made up of people. In the Church all are welcome. None are required to get a psychological exam before becoming a member. What follows are some clear guidelines that if implemented can go far toward reducing the possibility that the toxic element in your congregation can attack. However, as every priest in this study can witness, if motivated, the antagonists will not let anything stop them.

The Grinch Will Steal Christmas
The lion instinctively knows that if it is to successfully slay a prey it needs to attack when the victim is most vulnerable. Antagonists appear to have this same instinct. The majority of the accelerated attacks on the clergy in this study were done during the months of December and January. These are months when rectors are most vulnerable. They have completed the start up of the new fall program and the recruitment of all the volunteers needed for them. They

are concluding the annual stewardship drive. They are putting together the budget for the coming year and often seeking year-end gifts to meet the budget in the current year.

Advent and Christmas require tremendous preparation with additional programs and services. Then there is the preparation for the annual meeting which takes place most often soon after Christmas in the month of January. These are exhausting times for clergy. These are also busy times for parish leaders and the members of the congregation. If the clergy and parish leadership must also contend with the final shootout from the antagonists during this time there is often little energy left in them for the fight. The research for this book shows that either instinctively or deliberately the antagonists plan their major assault during December and January when the clergy and parish members are most vulnerable. In short, their intent is to steal Christmas.

The majority of the participants in this survey confessed to already being exhausted when the accelerated attacks began. **"No fight left". "Exhausted". "Burned out".** These were all phrases used to describe the way they felt. Just as the priest is called to pastor the parish, the parish also has a responsibility to nurture and care for the priest. A tired, worn out priest just going through the motions of ministry is as much a statement about the parish as it is about the priest's ability to set boundaries.

There are some things that a congregation can do to reduce the possibility that the antagonists might attack. What follows are some things that can help insure the health and energy of the senior pastor.

The Pre-Nuptial Agreement

Every senior pastor that is called to a congregation re-alizes that they will not be the last rector of that parish. Just as they have a first day they will also have a last day. It has become increasingly common for boards and senior pastors to have an employment contract or as we call them in the Episcopal Church, Letters of Mutual Agreement. While the agreement may contain many elements, I want to suggest several that are often overlooked but need to be included for the health of the priest, their family and the parish.

Two Consecutive Days Off

The concept of a priest having one day off a week, while Biblical in origin, is just not sufficient in today's Church with all the communication tools that virtually keep them available 24-7. Most clergy I know try to keep Friday as their *day off.* Fridays are also popular days for wedding rehears-als, dinners, socials and the beginning of weekend programs and retreats. In my thirty-eight years of parish ministry I could never identify with the TGIF slogan. Thanking God for Friday was not a part of my life experience. In addition to the many events that often interrupted my Friday there was the sermon I was to preach on Sunday that was never far from my thoughts.

I strongly recommend that clergy have as a part of their agreement that they will be given two consecutive days off per week. It wasn't until my third decade of ministry that I was able to figure a way to make that work. It was clearly understood in the parishes I served that my days off would begin after the last service on Sunday morning. I would re-turn to the parish at 1:00 p.m. on the following Tuesday.

Of course, if there were parish emergencies or funerals I would augment my schedule. This actually worked to insure that I could have some quality time with my children. It often meant that I had to take them out of school (to the utter dismay of their teachers) so that we could have time together. Otherwise, I was never able to be a part of the father-child activities that occur on weekends. I was working. The parish also learned that a rested priest was a lot more valuable to them than one that was worn out. Clergy are in a much better position to manage the attacks of the antagonists for the health of the congregation if they are not exhausted going into the battle.

Comp Time

What if the parish demands are such that a clergy person is not able to take their day off or even several days off in a row? It happens more often than not. Comp time is a common arrangement in the corporate world. These are paid days given to compensate for the days missed. For clergy this is especially true during Lent, Advent, and Christmas. Comp time needs to be included in the letter of agreement.

Sabbaticals

It is quite common for denominations to have sabbatical policies. Most state that the clergy earn two weeks sabbatical time for each year of service. I've read several that make the time available after three years and mandated every five years. Observation has taught me that taking the sabbatical time is not always so easily achieved. The time is seldom right in the life of the parish for the priest to be absent two to three months at a time. Then I read a Letter of Agreement that stated simply that the priest was to be compensated at their current salary and benefit level for any sabbatical time not taken. Such a clause in every agreement could do much to insure that clergy are encouraged to take the sabbatical time they've earned.

Continuing Education

None of us would think of purchasing an automobile or home and not maintain them. By the same token, continuing education is a vital part of keeping our clergy informed and growing so that they can be even more effective. Rare is the priest that will tell you that they learned everything they needed to know in seminary. Every year clergy should be given at least one full week to attend continuing education seminars. A part of this agreement should be a continuing education allowance that is included in the parish budget.

Sabbaticals must not be confused with continuing education. Sabbatical time must not be contingent on continuing to study and keeping a schedule. Sabbatical time is time to let the mind and body rest. Continuing education is the time given for additional study.

Annual Mutual Ministry Review

This too has become a common clause in most Letters of Agreement for clergy. The problem is that it is not defined. **The vestry often reads it as an opportunity to do a performance review of the rector.** I've even seen some instruments that simply utilize a point system to let the priest know "how he is doing".

The concept of a ministry review is that it should be mutual. The implication is that priest and people are engaged in a mutual ministry. The priest has not been employed by the parish to do ministry to and for them. They are not passive participants who sit in the pews alternately applauding and booing the priest as though he is the only performer in the arena.

A ministry review is mutual. The priest and the leadership agree on ministry goals for the rector. The senior pastor and the board agree on ministry goals for each member of the vestry and their respective committees. At the end of the year, they sit together, ideally with an outside consultant, and evaluate just what they did well, what needs improving, what was left undone that still needs to be done. It is also a time to add any additional goals for the coming year. That is a ministry evaluation that moves a parish forward. The Letter of Agreement between a rector and the vestry must not only include that there will be an annual review, but the nature of that review needs to be defined as well.

Dissolution Clause

Most every Letter of Agreement includes a clause that states that once signed, the agreement cannot be amended except by the mutual consent of the rector and vestry. In light of the current climate I would like to recommend one more clause. This clause would include the following details. That if the governing board should pursue a dissolution action against the rector, then any and all legal expenses resulting from that action incurred by the rector or the parish shall paid for by the vestry.

Then, I would recommend one further clause. It should be clearly agreed at the beginning that if the governing board initiates the dissolution of ministry action, the rector shall receive a minimum severance package. Depending on the size of the parish this should be a minimum of eighteen months and for larger parishes where the job possibilities for a removed priest are fewer it could go up to five years salary and benefits.

As has already been seen by our survey data, **a removed priest has a difficult time finding a new position even though they have done nothing wrong.** For most clergy it may take eighteen months or longer. While such a clause may appear harsh, based on my studies I think it could go some distance to give a governing board pause before initiating such an action. I would especially recommend a dissolution clause in the Letter of Agreement before accepting the call to serve a parish that has removed a previous senior pastor.

Consultants

The well-known quote states "he who is always his own counselor will often have a fool for his client". It is the wise rector that uses an outside consultant. Ideas can be filtered and conflict can be resolved. My own experience is that the consultant is best utilized to help put preventive measures in place that can help avoid conflict. If conflict does occur, the earlier the consultant is brought into the mix the greater the chance for a successful resolution. Once the conflict has reached the top of the pyramid the hope for a happy resolution through the use of a consultant is greatly diminished.

The majority of the clergy in this study did employ a consultant. **In none of the twenty-five cases was a consultant able to stop the antagonists from achieving their goal.** The consultants were able to change the tenor of the conversation for a time. They were able to equip the parish leadership with the needed conflict management tools to deal with the antagonists. Basically, the clergy that used the consultants were able to remain in their positions with the conflict subdued for another one to five years. The median amount of time a consultant was able to keep the antagonists underground was sixteen months. Conceivably this could give the perceptive rector capable of reading the handwriting on the wall time to search for another position.

Follow up interviews also showed that clergy that used a consultant received severance packages nearly triple those of the clergy that sought to negotiate the package on their own or rely on their bishop to do so. Severance packages negotiated by consultants averaged eighteen months to three years stipend. Those negotiated without the use of a consultant seldom exceeded six months salary and benefits.

The reality is that while a consultant can send the antagonists "underground" for a period of time by raising the awareness in the **healthy** parish leadership, the antagonists do not cease to be active. As one priest stated it so clearly, "during the time the vestry was working with the consultant my antagonists were quiet. What I realized later was that they had simply used the time to go out into the wilderness and find more recruits to fight with me."

Attorneys

Any senior pastor caught in an irresolvable conflict should not hesitate to consult an attorney. The majority of the clergy surveyed did employ an attorney. Most felt the need to do so to protect themselves and their families. Several reported that their attorneys did advise them that they had legal grounds to sue their antagonists for slander and defamation. Some are still considering the merits of such a suit. As the ministries of faithful and competent clergy continue to be brought to an end by antagonists such suits may in fact become a reality.

Most all the clergy that employed an attorney used that attorney to review their termination agreement and any **"hold harmless"** agreement the parish tried to thrust upon them. The use of an attorney is an expensive proposition. More than one priest surveyed suggested that a "Clergy Defense Fund" should be established by denominational leaders and made available for all clergy to use in these situations.

Questions for Discussion and Reflection

1. If you've ever been in a parish that removed a rector, did it occur during the months of December or January? Do you think that was planned or coincidental? Why or why not?

2. How do you feel about the author's contention that clergy should receive two consecutive days off in a given week? Have you ever given any thought to what a weekend looks like for your priest? Describe it.

3. What was your initial reaction to the idea of Comp Time? Do you know any companies that do this? Is it a part of your senior pastor's agreement?

4. Do you know the Biblical basis for taking a sabbatical? When was the last time your rector had a sabbatical? What do you think they should do on a sabbatical?

5. Does your parish budget include an allowance for the rector's continuing education? Why or why not?

6. Does your governing board and senior pastor conduct an annual mutual ministry review? What does the process include? Do they employ an outside consultant to guide them? Should they?

7. Respond to the concept of the Dissolution Clause recommended by the author. What do you like about it? What don't you like about it? Why or why not?

"The elders who direct the affairs of the church well are worthy of double honor, especially those whose work is preaching and teaching."
I Timothy 5:17

Chapter 7
An Audit is Not Enough

Attacking the financial operations of a parish is a favorite target for antagonists. If they can successfully plant seeds of doubt or raise enough smoke to suggest a fire, they have succeeded. While the governing board is the ultimate fiduciary in a parish, the senior pastor will be held accountable for any suggestions of impropriety. For that very reason every parish must go to the extreme to insure total and complete disclosure. The financial operations of the congregation must be beyond reproach.

So you have outside auditors conduct a professional audit of your financial records each year. Guess what? That's not enough! With all due respect to our many fine auditing firms would it surprise you to know that trainees often conduct parish audits? Church boards are notorious for looking for a bargain. They often seek out auditors that will give them the lowest price. While this is admirable on the surface, what needs to be acknowledged is that in order to secure an audit at the bargain price the firm often sends their trainees to conduct the audit.

It took me several years of working with auditors to realize that the Auditor's Management Letter is often no more than the dictated concerns of the head of the school, business manager, or parish treasurer. Trainees look to the person working most closely with them on the audit to flag the concerns for them that should be included in the Management Letter.

I served one congregation in which I caught the business administrator transferring 150,000 dollars out of a trust fund that was known only to him into his personal checking account. The vestry employed a highly effective and thorough forensic auditor. He uncovered multiple transactions into the business manager's personal funds. The auditing firm had missed all of these, but how?

Once again, the obvious had been missing. **The auditors can only audit the financial records they are given to audit.** A volunteer or employee of the parish embezzling funds is clever enough to know not to show the auditors the financial records that could expose them. They often keep two sets of books. One they show the governing body and the other they give to the auditors to audit. The final audit report is routinely not presented for six to eight months after the audit itself has been conducted. Rare is the board member or priest that will compare the financial statements revealed in the audit with the ones they received in last year's meetings. Such practices surrounding the parish audit are the perfect cover for a thief!

I am not suggesting that a parish not conduct professional audits. I think they should be mandated. **What I am suggesting is that every governing board have a standing committee known as the audit committee.** It should be made up of persons with financial expertise i.e., C.E.O.s, C.F.O.s, bankers, accountants, and bookkeepers. They must be the primary interface with the auditors and not the parish treasurer, business manager, head of school, or senior pastor. It is this audit committee that must actively oversee the audit and the writing of the Management Letter. They then are charged with reviewing the audit against the financial statements that were given to the governing board. It is the audit committee that should present the audit to the governing board.

So You Think You Have Internal Controls

One of the first visitors I had in my new parish was the volunteer treasurer. I'll never forget his statement. **"I could walk out of this building with a hundred dollars in my pocket every week and no one would ever know."** He'd been the C.F.O of a large corporation. He'd tried to raise red flags with the previous rector, but he'd rebuffed him stating that he was only concerned with the spiritual affairs of the parish. The treasurer had raised some questions with the governing board, but once again he'd been rebuffed. The money counters and the parish bookkeeper had all been members of the congregation for decades. The vestry trusted them to do their job. There was no reason to change the way they'd been doing things.

This is how it worked. There were two services on Sunday morning. The ushers passed the plates. The plates were presented at the altar and then placed on a side table. After the service the altar guild member on duty would empty the plates into a cloth moneybag and put the bag in a locked drawer in the sacristy. After the second service, in which the same process had been followed, the head usher would take the moneybags over to the parish bookkeeper's office. He'd lock them in a filing cabinet drawer. There they would remain until the next morning.

The bookkeeper would arrive early on Monday along with three to four volunteer money counters. The money counters would each take some of the contents of each bag and go to their respective card tables that had been set up in the hall. There they would individually tally the checks, cash and coins they had in their possession. They'd then return these to the bookkeeper who would then add up all the tally sheets and make out the deposit slip. On her lunch hour she would take the deposit to the bank.

How many opportunities for temptation did you see in the process? One of the most critical tasks for the audit committee is to set up internal controls for the parish. Once they are implemented the audit committee must work diligently to insure that they are being followed. The internal controls must be monitored and monitored and monitored.

The administrator that pled guilty to embezzling parish funds was able to steal from the parish by controlling the mail. He'd left strict instructions under penalty of dismissal with the receptionist that no one but him was to open the daily mail. All mail was to be locked up in a secure location until she could hand it over to him. That way he had direct control of all checks, financial statements, and trust documents sent to the parish. He'd even set up the bank accounts to be addressed to him personally and not the customary Rector, Wardens, and Vestry of said parish.

Implementing internal controls in the parish must begin from the moment a contribution is made. At no time should the tithes of the Faithful be left to the custodial care of one person. Every check should have at least two signatures on it. And the person responsible for accounting for the expenditures should **never** be one of those signatures.

Clergy Funds

Most every congregation has a system set up that allows clergy to administer funds in limited amounts independent of the governing board's direct approval. There are usually four such funds.

1. A discretionary or alms fund which is intended for confidential assistance to persons in need.

2. A continuing education fund for the clergy's ongoing education, books, and periodicals.

3. An expense or entertainment allowance for parish entertaining and expressions of appreciation to staff and volunteers.

4. Rector's funds which are used for projects and programs in addition to those provided by the budget.

A favorite target of antagonists is one of these clergy funds. They delight in the possibility of raising doubts or questions around the accounts that are directly under the control of the clergy. Even if a member of the clergy administers the funds in strict compliance with the policies governing them and have them audited, the antagonists can raise questions about the appropriateness of one or more of the expenditures. **The objection is usually around "how" they were spent, not that there was any wrongdoing.**

The antagonists can raise objections to the nature of the continuing education experience. *Was it really an educational experience or just an excuse for a vacation at parish expense?* I remember when the vestry approved funds for me to accompany two engineers from my parish to Haiti, arguably the poorest country in the Western Hemisphere. The purpose of the trip was to study the feasibility of installing a water system in a remote village. While there I assisted the engineers, taught in the diocesan seminary, met with the bishop, and toured the mission work that our parish and diocese was doing in that country. I could then return to the parish and promote our mission outreach from an informed standpoint. The antagonists in the parish critiqued the trip at great length as a Caribbean vacation at parish expense.

The point is that even if the governing board authorizes the expenditures, that will not protect a senior pastor from the attacks of the antagonists. Some of their favorite expressions are, "poor judgment" and "inappropriate expenditures". These words will be applied to everything from visiting lecturers or preachers you choose to invite to the way a rector entertains the staff at the annual Christmas party.

Still, it is essential that the policies governing each of the funds under the senior pastor's control be clearly and publicly stated. It is my preference that the offices of the Bishop audit these funds independently. A letter should be issued annually that the funds have been administered according to their stated purposes. That letter should be made a matter of public record.

If the diocese is unable or unwilling to do an audit of the rector's funds then the rector should **insist** that the senior warden and treasurer conduct said audit and issue a letter. Again, my preference is that the Bishop does this, especially if money has been given to provide confidential assistance to members of the parish in need. Clergy need to insist on the audit of these funds for their own protection.

Greatest Vulnerability

This study can easily conclude that the most fertile field for antagonists to sow their seeds of division is the financial one. For this reason, all the parish finances must be an open book. The manner in which the governing board monitors the parish finances should be a matter of public record. There can be **no secrets!** While many clergy don't like having their salaries made a matter of public record, our compensation along with that of all the staff needs to be made readily available to the parish. But they must always be presented **in context.** Every three years the finance committee should conduct a compensation study with similar sized parishes. The compensation packages of rectors to sextons should be presented in the context of what comparable positions are paid. When presented as a line item in the budget, there is always room for speculation and objection. When presented in the context of what other rectors in similar parishes with similar responsibilities receive, the field for objection is less fertile.

A Word of Caution to the Clergy

I remember taking some questions I had about a particular parish bookkeeper to my bishop at the time. He looked at me very sternly, "You must avoid the temptation to act like a corporate C.E.O. You are a priest! You need to focus on the spiritual affairs of the parish. Leave the temporal and financial to the vestry." A couple of weeks later I turned the corner into that bookkeeper's office and saw her stuffing several hundred dollars into her purse. The parish moneybag was open on her desk. I retrieved the cash and terminated the employment of the bookkeeper. I advised the bishop and the vestry of my action and the reasons for it.

My sisters and brothers of the collar, **we cannot abdicate our responsibility for the temporal and financial affairs of the parish in the name of the spiritual.** If the vestry is not doing its job, you must be their conscience. If strict internal controls are not in place, then for our own sake and that of the parish we must see that they are implemented and insist that the vestry monitor them. To do otherwise is to leave our parish and ourselves wide open to the destructive work of the antagonists.

Questions for Discussion and Reflection

1. Does your parish have a system of internal controls reviewed annually and monitored by an audit committee?

2. Trace a cash donation placed in the offering plate to the bank step by step in your parish. Are there always at least two people overseeing the gift?

3. Now do so with a check sent to your parish in the mail. Does the same apply? Do you have a different person opening the bank statements than the person that reconciles them?

4. Are there two signatures on all parish checks?

5. Are all your bank accounts designated in the name of the Rector, Wardens, and Vestry?

6. How are the funds entrusted to the clergy audited each year?

7. What is the best way to handle complaints from antagonists that they disagree with some of the expenditures a priest has authorized?

PART FIVE
WHAT NEEDS TO HAPPEN?

"If another member of the church sins against you, go and point out the fault when the two of you are alone. If the member listens to you, you have regained that one. But if you are not listened to, take one or two others along with you so that every word may be confirmed by two witnesses. If the member refuses to listen to them, tell it to the church; and if the offender refuses to listen even to the church, let such a person be to you as a Gentile and a tax collector."

Matthew 18:15-17

Chapter 8
If Only…

Absolutely every clergy person in our study was in agreement that **the one thing that could have changed everything was a strong intervention by his or her bishop.** This did not happen in any of the case studies. Half of the priests surveyed reported that they believed their bishops had almost immediately sided with the antagonists. They reported that their bishops actively worked with the antagonists for their removal. Some of the bishops turned on the priests completely, attacking them verbally, sending them for psychological evaluation, investigating the priest's past ministries or threatening to "defrock" them as being unfit for ministry.

"I didn't even know that my Bishop was involved until I received a telephone call from him. He just started shouting at me over the telephone. He was blaming me for all the problems in the parish." Another priest wrote, "It was as though he was only willing to listen to the loudest voices". And yet another, "He didn't even ask me for my point of view. He assumed everything that the antagonists had told him about me was true". Yet another wrote, "I couldn't even get my Bishop to return my telephone calls. The antagonists, on the other hand, were in and out of his office on a daily basis". And one more, "My wardens and I tried to talk to him to explain that there were just a handful of folks that were causing problems and that their opinions were not those of the majority of the parish. He told my Wardens that those folks were not troublemakers. He knew them personally. They *were faithful members of the congregation that only wanted what was best for the parish.* He insisted that the only way there could be peace in the parish again was for me to leave."

Several of the priests reported that when the antagonists attacked them **their bishops simply didn't know how to respond to them.** One of our participants wrote, "The Bishop and the Canon were both supportive on the telephone, but they never followed through on their promises to help me. I was left to fight with the antagonists alone." A few of the bishops did confront the antagonists and asked them to stop, but when the antagonists refused the bishop simply removed himself from any further involvement in the process. In one case, the antagonists at a public meeting of the congregation verbally attacked their bishop and the bishop was shouted down any time he attempted to speak. In another the bishop was so visibly shaking at the confrontation he needed to be comforted by the rector and his supporters.

The most common methods used by the bishops were to try to broker a ministry compromise with the antagonists. When that failed, as it did in each case in our study, the bishop would encourage the priest to look for a new position, resign, or if possible, retire. Ultimately, all the bishops in our study had to agree to the terms of the dissolution of ministry agreements in order for the participants in our survey to resign or retire. The antagonists were victorious. Remember, their goal from the beginning was the removal of the priest.

This Does Work

When I began this study, my preconceived idea was that clergy serving in denominations with an authoritative hierarchy would have the advantage in dealing with antagonists. Those serving parishes that elect their senior pastor by congregational vote would have a distinct disadvantage. At first glance, one would think that a priest under attack by a handful of dissidents need only call the denominational office and the appropriate authority would come to the rescue. This study has dispelled that notion.

But I didn't want to leave it there. **So I actively began to look for cases where the bishop did play a positive role in the priest's battle with antagonists**. I realized that in my forty years of ministry I only had personal knowledge of two cases when a bishop took a strong stand with antagonists. In both cases, the respective bishops met with them, listened to them, and then counseled that since they were so unhappy in their current parish they needed to move to another. In both cases the bishop presented the antagonists with signed letters of membership transfer and told them they could take their membership to any parish in his diocese and they would be welcomed, but they were no longer members of their current parish. In one of those cases the bishop also insisted that a much beloved, but troublesome retired priest relocate as well. A leading layman in one of those congregations told me, **"the Sunday after that group of bullies left even the bricks in this building breathed more easily."**

Fifteen years ago I had a conversation with a friend that had just been ordained as a bishop. He made the statement that he'd already let the lay leadership in his diocese know that he would not tolerate having clergy abused in his diocese. The bishop retired recently. I telephoned him and asked if during his tenure any rector had been removed from his parish against his will in his diocese. His answer, "None".

He did report that he enabled two dissolutions, but they were not the result of clergy under attack, but a realization by both priest and congregation that they were not right for each other. He then gave me the names of several clergy in his former diocese that had appealed to him for help when they were under attack. He suggested that I contact them and hear what they had to say. He made it clear that he did all the conflict management in his diocese. He did not farm it out.

Each of the priests I contacted could have repeated any one of the stories revealed in one of the twenty-five case studies. The names would only need to be changed but the behavior and the characteristics of those leading the charge against the priest were the same. Each had been under attack by a handful of people in their congregations. The scenario was the same. These small bands had high control needs and were very angry. They resented the priest and became increasingly malicious in their attacks as the struggle continued.

When the priests contacted my bishop friend and asked him to stand behind them and support them, his response was, **"I will not only stand behind you, I am going to stand with you."**

Another priest stated, "I felt like I was a true teammate with my Bishop. **We were in a joint venture to keep the parish healthy.** I always knew that when I telephoned him if he didn't pick up the phone immediately he'd get back to me within twenty-four hours."

The Classic Tools of Conflict Management

The Bishop then utilized the most classic tools in conflict management. **But he used them with all the force and authority of his office.** That is something no conflict management consultant can do. First, there would be **no triangulation** and second, there would be **nothing anonymous.** No triangulation meant that the Bishop would never meet with the antagonists without the Rector and his two wardens also being present. No anonymous sources or comments would be allowed. They were off the table. People had to own their own stuff.

The Bishop made it clear from the onset that he was there to support the priest, but he also wanted to be a pastor to those that were unhappy. When meeting with them in his office or at a special vestry meeting to hear their grievances, the Bishop continually asked them to help him understand why they were so unhappy. He never accused the people of bad behavior. He tried to stay positive. He set as the end goal for each meeting that everyone would leave happy. He tried to find a win–win. His favorite question was, **"What can we do to make you happy?"**

If a person became unruly the Bishop would challenge them. "You are not being helpful so sit down and be quiet until you have something constructive to offer". When it became apparent that their objective was to remove the priest and that nothing short of that would make them happy. The Bishop would firmly remind them that he was the Bishop of the diocese and the rector was there to stay.

Once the antagonists understood that they could not triangulate with the bishop the struggle would come to an end. As for the antagonists, in each parish they simply went away. Some joined another parish and some simply disappeared from the parish scene.

As for the parishes that the antagonists left, they continue to grow and are filled with vitality. They are thriving parishes attracting new members and bringing converts to Christ. One of the priests reported that not only did their parish experience a growth in numbers and stewardship but they had successfully weathered some difficult renovation projects to their historic property. **"I told my Bishop that the reason I've been successful in this place is because I've had a great Bishop to work with."**

Any visitor to one of these congregations would conclude that they are communities of deep spirituality and renewal. One can only speculate what the condition of these parishes would be today if the antagonists had successfully removed these clergy and divided the congregation. But then again, based on twenty-five case studies, one can only conclude that taking a parish back to its stagnant state is what the antagonists want most.

A Change In Governance

An interesting footnote in one of these parish scenarios is that prior to the struggle the parish elected the two wardens. After the struggle they revised their by-laws to allow the rector to choose the senior warden and the vestry to elect from their number the junior warden.

Spiritual Warfare

As for the priests each acknowledged that they felt like they had been in a spiritual warfare. One observed, **"if Satan wants to hurt the Body of Christ he needs only recruit a handful of resentful people and have them attack the leadership and divide the congregation."** They each are so grateful that they had a bishop that understood this and that he was willing to stand with them.

I asked each of them if they thought their antagonists saw themselves as evil? All agreed that their antagonists were so filled with anger and resentment they were unable to own their stuff. That observation both summarizes and completes the profile of an antagonist.

I once heard Rabbi Friedman, the author of *Generation to Generation* (Guildford Press), speak to a gathering of private school administrators. When asked how to best respond to difficult personalities that insisted on creating havoc in their schools, Rabbi Friedman's response was blunt and direct. He stated, **"Sometimes the only way to deal with these people is for the person in authority to say to them emphatically, Knock it off!"**

Conclusions

Our participant's case studies demonstrate a pattern that denominational authorities, clergy, and lay leaders simply must take into consideration. Beyond consideration, there are some **Red Flags** that demand that for the health of clergy, their families and the congregations these flags cannot be ignored. Those responsible for calling or assigning senior pastors need to resolve these issues as a part of the calling process. Based on these twenty-five case studies, the following conclusions can be drawn.

1. There are controlling, angry personalities in congregations that find their fulfillment by attacking and destroying clergy.

2. Congregations that have allowed the antagonists to unseat a previous senior pastor will most likely do it again.

3. All but one case indicated that the antagonists were being led by an active or retired member of the clergy team in the parish. Assisting clergy that had made political pastoral alliances in the congregation were the most dangerous.

4. Neighboring clergy and/or the senior pastor's current or previous bishop often assisted the antagonists. This was especially true when theological or political differences existed between the bishop and the rector.

5. This bishops and denominational authorities in our case studies were ill equipped to deal with conflict led by antagonists.

6. The most successful method for dealing with antagonists is when all the players in the system refuse to allow the antagonists to triangulate and utilize anonymous sources.

Antagonists Do Exist

The Church is designed to be a loving, accepting and forgiving community. It is difficult for us to accept that there are members that have no remorse about attacking clergy and dividing congregations. The work in this area concludes beyond a shadow of a doubt that this is a luxury we can no longer afford.

It would be charitable to observe that the antagonists in our midst are ill. Perhaps they do suffer from Narcissistic Personality Disorder. Our study also indicates that they may simply be controlling personalities that have refused to do their own spiritual work of self-examination. Or, one could conclude that they are alcoholic personalities refusing treatment or skipping steps in their own recovery. It is likely that a small fraction is emotionally unstable people that could benefit from treatment. Our efforts at diagnosing and being charitable will be to no avail if they are allowed to continue to attack and destroy. Bishops and parish leaders that allow them to do so must distinguish between **being enablers for those that enjoy bullying the clergy** and forgiving pastors.

Don't Ignore the Parish History

All the work in this area, as limited as it is, concludes beyond doubt that a parish that has removed a previous pastor will be inclined to do it again. Clergy candidates for these congregations must not delude themselves into believing *that they will be the exception.* As has been seen by this study, the twenty-five participants are all extremely gifted clergy. They were sought after and served some of the most enviable congregations in the American Church. Even the congregations with this history thrived under their leadership. **They were targeted not because the parish was failing under their leadership, but in each instance the parish was thriving.**

Denominational authorities need to work with congregations that have this DNA in their history. The clauses I suggested in the Letters of Agreement will not only protect the new senior pastor but help the leaders of he congregation take a hard look at their own history. Even if the toxic element of the congregation has been silent for several years or decades this study shows that once a congregation has removed a senior pastor they will do it again.

An Untouchable Staff or Clergy Person

Our study concludes that this one factor, more than any other, may determine whether or not the antagonists spring into action against a given rector. Denominational authorities, search committees, and candidates for the rector's position seldom include it in the equation. Yet, once again this just may be the **biggest red flag** of all. If such a staff person has played an active role in the removal of a previous senior pastor, then they need to be removed by the appropriate authorities before a new senior pastor is even announced.

By the same token, if there exists a staff person that exercises a pastoral ministry that could potentially exclude a new rector from having that role, they too need to be removed. If at any time there is a staff person that begins to "stir up the sheep" in opposition to the rector they need to be removed immediately!

Political Mean Spiritedness

One only has to watch any television station, regardless of political leanings, to discover one or more commentators making very "mean spirited" comments about members of the opposing political party. More than one of the clergy in this study made the observation that this same destructive spirit is quite evident in the Church of Jesus Christ.

Bishops and clergy are often at odds with one another over the ordination of women and the roles that gay and lesbian persons should have in the Church. I am writing this manuscript at a time in the American Church when the economy is faltering and many still fear on the verge of collapse. Rectors and governing boards are having to make difficult and often painful decisions about expenditures. Disagreements over how Church funds should be used permeate most every congregation. Conflict is an inevitable part of that. **Search committees desperately seek savior Rectors while resident rectors become lightning rods for the frustrated.**

While it is not what any faithful Christian wants to hear it still has to be said. Some bishops and clergy have and are being used by antagonists in their efforts to bring down their rectors. This is especially true when there are vast theological or political differences between a rector and her bishop or a rector and his fellow clergy.

A Firm Hand Is Needed

Bishops and denominational authorities simply must utilize the authority that is theirs by virtue of office when dealing with personalities intent on hurting clergy and dividing congregations. The fact that only a couple of the bishops in our survey even bothered to check with the clergy and the healthy parish leadership to determine if the accusations of the antagonists were true speaks volumes. The antagonists in all but a few of our case studies were able to get the bishop to triangulate against the rector and to use anonymous sources and innuendo to fuel the fire. It is even more condemning to realize that the majority of the denominational authorities in this study either joined forces with the antagonists or chose to remain passive.

It must be observed that many clergy elected to the office of bishop simply may not have been trained in the basic tools of conflict management. If this is the case, then they will be ill equipped to deal with the conflict methods of the antagonists. It also needs to be observed that many clergy elected to this office are gentle souls that prefer peace at all costs. Many are introverted personalities that tend to withdraw from confrontations and aggressive personalities. **The conclusions of this study certainly suggest that the bishops and denominational authorities in these twenty-five case studies did not possess the needed tools to manage the conflicts with the antagonists.** They appear to have been equally ill equipped to deal with clergy both active and retired that triangulate with the antagonists in order to unseat a senior pastor.

Since the study further concludes that these personalities do exist in our Church those in authority must develop the tools for dealing with them. This needs to be done for the health of the clergy and the congregations they shepherd. An important metaphor to recall is that of the shepherd's crook or staff. Every bishop is given one when they are ordained. It has two ends to it. Both have a function. Our bishops must be trained on how to use both ends!

Candidates for new positions in a diocese need to spend as much effort determining the qualities of their new bishop as they do the parish itself. Will the new bishop stand with them if antagonists in the parish decide to act? Does that bishop have a history of defending their clergy? These are questions that can usually only be answered by asking current and former clergy in a given diocese. This is a piece of research clergy candidates must not neglect. Do not get caught up in the emotion of being romanced by a new parish. Don't lie to yourself. What happened to the twenty-five clergy and their congregations in this book could just as easily happen to you and to your parish. There are hundreds if not thousands of clergy in the Church that thought they would be the exception. Most of the clergy in this study thought so as well. They weren't!

Triangulation and Anonymous Rumors

Even if a rector or a bishop is not trained in conflict management two simple covenants can have very positive results. In order to begin to neutralize those that delight in bullying clergy, **the bishop of any diocese needs only to make it public that they will not tolerate triangulation or anonymous rumors.** If a member wants to complain about their rector they need to bring the rector with them to the bishops office to voice their complaint.

This same practice needs to be implemented in the parish. **Wardens and vestry members must remove themselves from being "mouth pieces" for the discontented.** If a member telephones them with a complaint about their rector, the board member should insist that the member go with them to see the rector to directly verbalize their complaint. Otherwise, they simply don't want to hear it. Triangulation does nothing but build up irreconcilable conflict that cannot be resolved without the virtual destruction of another person's livelihood and reputation.

A similar covenant must be reached regarding **anonymous rumors**. Repeatedly in this study the clergy reported that anonymous rumors were used against them. Sadly and to my surprise several of the clergy reported that the anonymous rumors were repeated by their own bishop or a member of the diocesan staff. These insinuations were often veiled in a cloud of secrecy. The anonymity of their source was protected with this or a similar sentence, "**We know something about your priest, but we can't tell you.**" Such insinuations are far more damaging to a priest's reputation than an actual accusation. When insinuations are presented in that package the content can only be filled with wild imagination and speculation.

Several of the clergy reported that they didn't even learn that one of their diocesan executives was making these unsubstantiated insinuations about them until after they had left the parish. Even then they were unable to rebut the rumors since no details were revealed. Such statements are not only inflammatory and difficult to refute, but quite honestly as one of our participants observed – **"they are downright cowardly."** It would be more accurate to name such statements for exactly what they are and immediately question both the statement and **the motives** of the person making them. By verbalizing such statements to search committees and church boards the bishops and diocesan executives are either knowingly or intentionally being used by the antagonists to do their work for them.

By removing the weapons of triangulation and anonymous rumors from the voices of the antagonists much can be done in congregations and dioceses to disarm them. Our first concern must always be for the health of our clergy and the congregations they serve. Jesus did instruct us in a charitable and direct method for dealing with our grievances against one another. Triangulation and anonymous rumors that led to his own crucifixion are not a part of his instructions.

In Shakespeare's Othello Act 3, scene 3, Iago makes this statement, "Good name in man and woman, dear my lord. Is the immediate jewel of their souls. Who steals my purse steals trash; 'tis something, nothing; 'Twas mine, 'tis his, and has been slave to thousands. But he that filches from me my good name robs me of that which not enriches him and makes me poor indeed. **It must be understood that antagonists not only want to rob their clergy target of their purse, but their good name as well.**

ॐॐ

Questions for Discussion and Reflection

1. Has the governing board of your parish made a covenant in writing to rule as "out of order" all anonymous rumors and gossip? Is it working?

2. Has your governing board made a covenant in writing with the senior pastor not to allow members to triangulate? All concerns will be expressed in the presence of the senior pastor. Is it renewed annually?

3. Does your rector and vestry have this same covenant not to be a party to triangulation with your bishop and diocesan officers?

4. Do you think your bishop would be willing to be the conflict manager for your rector if the need should arise? Would the bishop "stand with" your rector?

5. How would you respond to a statement like this, "We have some disturbing information about your senior pastor, but we can't share it with you?" What if your bishop or a member of her staff made that statement?

PART SIX
LIFE BEYOND THE TOXIC PARISH

How beautiful are the feet of them that preach the gospel of peace, and bring glad tidings of good things!
Romans 10:15

Chapter 9
Getting Your Life Back

Interim Ministry Rescue

Only three priests of the twenty-five in our study received calls as rectors to a new parish after going through this experience. Two more were called to be associates in very large congregations and ironically with greater compensation than they'd received as rectors. Two were called to positions in a diocesan office far removed from the one they left. Two more took retirement and two more retired after being certified with a medical disability.

The overwhelming majority began new ministries as professional interim ministers. For clergy that have been attacked by antagonists, it appears that interim ministry may just be the best avenue for them to pursue. Interim ministers serve normally only one to two years in a parish before moving on to the next one. For clergy who want to continue in full time ministry after battling with the antagonists, this is probably the safest way they can continue to serve the Church and have a fulfilling ministry. Some have done multiple interim assignments all over the United States. These ministries have not only provided a means to care for themselves and their families, but a safe way to continue to do those things that they were ordained to do. But, sadly, a few of our survey participants reported their antagonists even attempted to disrupt interim assignments they had been given.

A Damning Judgment

The majority of our survey participants have been able to find wonderful lives beyond the trauma of being attacked by the antagonists. We already noted the one that that continues to suffer from such severe depression as to need continued hospitalization from time to time. Three of the participant's marriages ended in divorce. They directly attribute the strain placed on their marriages by the antagonists as a contributing factor. There were instances of spousal adultery that the spouses, justified or not, blame on the trauma with the antagonists. Reports of spouses that became addicted to prescription medicines prescribed during the experience were also documented.

Those diagnosed with Post Traumatic Stress Syndrome will most likely be plagued by nightmares for the greater portion of their lives. All our participants, spouses and children now have a more cynical attitude toward the Church and people. Most all confessed to continuing to have problems trusting others. The loss to the Church of spouses, children and lay members that formerly were faithful and enthusiastic about their lives in the Church is **a damning judgment on the work of the antagonists**. Several of the clergy in our study reported they keep their participation in Church life to a minimum.

Reinventing Yourself

Still, most all our participants report that they have been able to move on with their lives. As has already been stated some found new positions as rectors, associates, or on diocesan staffs. Others are enjoying the fruits of retirement, reconnecting with their spouses, children, and grandchildren. They report that there are opportunities for them to preach and lead liturgy, but it is their choice to participate or not.

One of the most revealing statements by one of our participants might best describe the feelings of most of the clergy in our study. "In a strange way leaving that parish was a gift that I am quite certain they didn't intend to give me. I feel like I've gotten my life back. Looking back I realize I'd become a one-dimensional person. That parish had become my entire life. I had no other interests. God forgive me but I'd even lost touch with my wife and children. Now I have a much fuller life with varied interests and friends. It would probably drive the people that attacked me crazy, but they actually gave my life back to me. **I feel just like Brer Rabbit. And thanks to them I am playing in a brand new briar patch."**

Tough Words of Encouragement

I have had to offer the following words of comfort and hope to several clergy that have chosen to end their battle with the antagonists. I want to conclude by repeating them here. **"Continuing the battle just may be your worst alternative.** To do so will only further divide your congregation. Fighting on will bring further stress and emotional suffering to your spouse and children. You need also to realize what this battle has done and is doing to you emotionally, spiritually, and physically."

"You need to realize that ending the battle does not mean that the antagonists will retreat. They very well may continue to attack you if you choose to seek other ministries. It is certain they will continue to defame your name whenever it is mentioned in the congregation after you leave. You and those you love will continue to suffer the emotional, spiritual, and mental consequences of having been attacked. But all of this is information about the antagonists. **It is not information about you."**

"You know that you did a good job. Your accomplishments speak for themselves. The fruits of the ministries that you put in place will continue on. The people that you counseled, prayed with, comforted, and blessed will never forget that you were there with them in their times of joy and need. Ninety-eight percent of the people you served appreciate you, love you, and will continue to do so long after you leave this place. God loves you. The Lord brought you to this parish to be a blessing. You were exactly that to those that allowed your ministry to bless them. **The condemnation rests on the heads of those that rejected you.** In Christ's own words they have rejected the one that He sent to them. In rejecting you they have rejected Him. Just remember, there is life beyond this parish. It just may be a better life than you ever thought possible."

"You did not choose me, but I chose you and appointed you to go and bear fruit that will last."
John 15:16

When Under Attack

Action Steps for a Clergy Person

If you have confidence that your Bishop will "stand with you", refuse to triangulate with the antagonists and rule all anonymous reports out of order, the first telephone call you need to make is to him or her. If they will use the weight of their office to manage the conflict in a supportive manner you need to read no further. If not, give some serious consideration to the next ten steps.

1. Do not get caught up in the anxiety. Communicate to the parish leadership that while you are aware of the "concerns" of the antagonists you plan to address them in an objective and factual manner. Enter a signed non-triangulation covenant with your board if you have not already done so.

2. Take extra steps to take care of yourself physically, emotionally, and spiritually. Get plenty of rest.

3. Insist that all conversations take place at the factual level of the conflict pyramid.

4. Keep the healthy leadership in the parish advised of the concerns of the antagonists and the way in which you want to address them. Ask for their advice and assistance.

5. Advise the denominational leader or bishop that you are aware of the antagonist's concerns and the methods you'd like to use to address them. Ask your bishop not to triangulate with the antagonists and to include your two wardens and yourself in all meetings with the antagonists. Ask him not accept anonymous complaints.

6. If the antagonists insist on using personal innuendo and accusation, bring in a consultant to help you redirect the dialogue and bring the antagonists into the open. Advise the antagonists that your spouse and children are "off limits" or you will take legal action against them.

7. If the consultant recommends that you begin looking for a new position, seriously consider their counsel.

8. If the antagonists begin directing their attacks toward your spouse or children, employ an attorney and make it known that you have employed an attorney.

9. If both you and the parish leadership should run out of energy for the fight and decide to dissolve your relationship, employ a consultant to negotiate your severance package. Have an attorney review it.

10. Refuse to sign a "Hold Harmless" agreement especially if some of the antagonists are members of the governing board. If the antagonists continue to try to destroy your future ministry and reputation, you may have to use litigation against them in order to get them to stop.

Action Steps for the Church Board

If you have confidence that your Bishop will "stand with you", refuse to triangulate with the antagonists and rule all anonymous reports out of order, the first telephone call you need to make is to him or her. If they will use the weight of their office to manage the conflict in a supportive manner you need to read no further. If not, give some serious consideration to the next ten steps.

1. The board leadership along with the senior pastor should meet with the antagonists and listen to their concerns. The wardens or board leadership should not meet with those who have complaints without the rector being present. The wardens need to advise the antagonists that they have a covenant of non-triangulation.

2. The pastor and vestry leadership together should make a plan for trying to address their concerns. The senior pastor and the wardens should meet with the bishop and ask her not to triangulate with the antagonists and not to listen to anonymous rumors or accusations.

3. The vestry leadership should try to determine the names of those seeking the removal of the rector and evaluate their spiritual and financial contributions to the parish.

4. If the antagonists refuse to accept the manner in which the concerns have been addressed and continue their attack on the priest, the leadership should once again meet with them and insist that they stop. They should let the antagonists know that they are aware of their financial stewardship.

5. If this fails the vestry needs to support the rector in choosing and working with a consultant.

6. If the consultant in unable to redirect the conversation with the antagonists then the rector and wardens should make one last appeal to the bishop or diocesan authority to deal firmly with the antagonists.

7. If the rector and leadership of the vestry decide that they have no fight left in them, the vestry should work with the rector to find an equitable severance package. It is important that the parish believes that the vestry has treated the departing rector with charity and fairness.

8. The vestry needs to have their own attorney review the dissolution or retirement agreement.

9. If none on the vestry have been a part of the group of antagonists, then the vestry should try to get the departing rector to agree to sign a "Hold Harmless" agreement with the individual members of the current vestry.

10. The board should host a celebration of the departing rector's ministry and make provision for those that have been loyal to him to express their appreciation.

∽∼

ABOUT THE AUTHOR

The Reverend Doctor Dennis R. Maynard is the author of ten books. Well over 100,000 Episcopalians have read his book, "Those Episkopols". 2500 congregations around the United States use "Those Episkopols" in their new member ministries. Several denominational leaders have called it the unofficial handbook for the Episcopal Church. He is also the author of "Forgive and Get Your Life Back" which has been used by the same number of clergy to do forgiveness training in their congregations. Maynard has written a series of novels focusing on life in the typical congregation. These novels have received popular acceptance from both clergy and lay people.

Over his thirty-eight years of parish ministry he has served some of the largest congregations in the Episcopal Church. His ministry included parishes in Illinois, Oklahoma, South Carolina, Texas, and California. President George H.W. Bush and his family are members of the congregation he served in Houston, Texas, also the largest parish in the Episcopal Church.

He has served other notable leaders that represent the diversity of his ministry. These national leaders include Former Secretary of State, James Baker; Former Secretary of Education, Richard Riley; Supreme Court Nominee, Clement Haynsworth; and the infamous baby doctor, Benjamin Spock, among others.

Doctor Maynard maintains an extensive speaking and travel schedule. He is frequently called on to speak, lead retreats, or serve as a consultant to parishes, schools and organizations throughout the United States.

His most recent endeavors are earning him a reputation as a novelist. The books in *The Magnolia Series* are growing in popularity around the nation as readers anxiously await each new chapter.

"The novels give us a chance to look at the underside of parish life. While the story lines are fictional, the readers invariably think they recognize the characters. If not, they know someone just like the folks that attend First Episcopal Church in the town of Falls City, Georgia."

Over his thirty-eight years of parish ministry Doctor Maynard served on various diocesan boards and committees. These included various diocesan program committees, director of summer camps for boys, diocesan trustee, finance committee, and executive committees. He was elected Dean of the diocesan deanery on several occasions. He was on the Cursillo secretariat and was spiritual director for the Cursillo Movement multiple times. Maynard served as co-chair for two diocesan capital campaigns.

In the National Episcopal Church he served multiple terms on the board of the National Association of Episcopal Schools and as a trustee for Seabury Western Theological Seminary. He was named an adjunct professor in congregational development at Seabury. Maynard was the co-coordinator for two national conferences for large congregations with multiple staff ministries.

Doctor Maynard was twice named to "Oxford's Who's Who The Elite Registry of Extraordinary Professionals" and to "Who's Who Among Outstanding Americans."

Maynard earned an Associate of Arts Degree in psychology, a Bachelor of Arts Degree in the social sciences, a Masters Degree in theology, and a Doctor of Ministry Degree. He currently resides in Rancho Mirage, California.

WWW.EPISKOPOLS.COM

BOOKS FOR CLERGY AND THE PEOPLE THEY SERVE

6697681R0

Made in the USA
Lexington, KY
14 September 2010